Child
Protection

SAGE COURSE COMPANIONS

KNOWLEDGE AND SKILLS *for* SUCCESS

RVC
LEARNING CENTRE

Child Protection

Eileen Munro

SAGE Publications

London ● Thousand Oaks ● New Delhi

SAGE Publications Ltd
1 Oliver's Yard
55 City Road
London EC1Y 1SP

SAGE Publications Inc.
2455 Teller Road
Thousand Oaks, California 91320

SAGE Publications India Pvt Ltd
B-42, Panchsheel Enclave
Post Box 4109
New Delhi 110 017

British Library Cataloguing in Publication data

A catalogue record for this book is available from
the British Library

ISBN-10 1-4129-1178-8   ISBN-13 978-1-4129-1178-8
ISBN-10 1-4129-1179-6 (pbk) ISBN-13 978 1-4129-1179-5 (pbk)

Library of Congress Control Number: 2006926137

Typeset by C&M Digitals (P) Ltd., Chennai, India
Printed on paper from sustainable resources
Printed in Great Britain by The Cromwell Press Ltd, Trowbridge, Wiltshire

contents

Every Child Matters, the government Green Paper published in 2003 (Treasury, 2003), sets out an ambitious plan of reform of children's services. The goal is to help all children fulfil their potential. Existing services have been criticised for having become too preoccupied with issues of serious, familial child abuse and neglect, paying too little attention to the needs of other children and the other welfare needs of abused children. Children's services have been undergoing major changes in organisational structures and work practices in an effort to transform the culture from a reactive service for a few to a preventive service for the many. It is hoped that all professionals in contact with children can become better at noticing low-level signs of concern in a child's health or development and at providing a constructive response to that concern so that it does not develop into a more serious problem.

Within this broader agenda, the area of work traditionally known as child protection still needs to be dealt with. This covers the problems in children's health and development caused by abuse and neglect. Children may be abused by others in their communities or by strangers, but the focus of child protection services has been predominantly on abuse by parents or carers. Children's services continue to have special duties in relation to children who are suffering or at risk of suffering significant harm. In many cases, the source of that harm will be abuse or neglect, usually within the home. The fact that the harm occurs within the home creates specific problems in helping the child since it affects the role of the parents. With most problems that a child has, the parents are the people with most concern to solve them and they can generally be trusted to be honest and to try to co-operate with professionals. However, if a parent is the source of danger, then their version of events may be misleading and their efforts at co-operation ambivalent at best.

If preventive services are effective in helping families there will be some reduction in the number that escalate to serious abuse or neglect. However, at this stage, it is too soon to know how big an impact the new children's services will have on reducing abuse and neglect and, of course, some cases of abuse do not follow the pattern of slow deterioration in family functioning. Therefore, for the foreseeable future, child abuse and neglect by parents and carers will continue to be significant problems for those working in children's services.

Child protection is one of the most worthwhile areas of work with children and parents since it can make a crucial difference to the quality of children's lives and, sometimes, it literally makes the difference between life and death. But it is also the most daunting and challenging.

Child abuse is an intrinsically hard problem to tackle. By its very nature, it is hard to see, with abusers often going to great lengths to conceal the harm they are doing to the child. Even once it has been identified, it is difficult to judge how serious it is, what degree of future risk there is, and what could be done to help the child. We have only a limited, and disputed, understanding of the causes of abusive behaviour and how to keep the child safe.

The work is not just intellectually but also emotionally challenging. An accusation of abuse, whether justified or not, stirs up strong reactions in most parents, of fear, anxiety, anger or shock. To accuse someone of being an abusive parent strikes at the very heart of their identity and sense of self-worth. Children who are being abused are psychologically scarred by it, making it hard for the social worker to gain their trust. The emotional impact on professionals themselves is another inevitable and complicating factor. Badly handled, this can distort their reasoning about a case as well as harming their own mental health, leading to burnout and a high turnover of staff.

In addition to the intrinsic complexities of the work, there are immense social pressures. No one can have failed to notice the strength of public reaction when a case goes tragically wrong and a child dies. The critical media stories, the naming and shaming of key workers, the rebukes from politicians, all combine to add to the stress of the work.

At the heart of good child protection work are expert professionals

The intense public concern has, not surprisingly, increased the priority given to improving practice and making children safer, leading to fundamental changes in the workplace in the past two decades. Central government and local management have provided ever more detailed rules and guidance on how the work should be done, accompanied by closer managerial oversight to ensure the guidance is followed. Child protection work is now under tighter political and managerial control than any other part of social work. Besides the legal framework setting out professionals' powers and duties, there are detailed guidelines, procedures, and standard assessment instruments prescribing how the work should be done.

With all this guidance available, the reader might question what this textbook can add. The London child protection procedures, for instance, now come in a 300-page book that weighs a kilo (London CPC, 2002). But, while it contains a wealth of valuable information, particularly about how to work with other professions, it only catches some features of practice.

It is important to see all the rules and guidance as *aids* to practice; they cannot *replace* the professional expertise of the individual worker who is actually working with the family. They cannot transform the task into a clerical process. Official procedures and assessment frameworks are essential elements in practice, but they need to be integrated with the professonal's reasoning skills, emotional intelligence and understanding of human nature and culture to lead to good-quality work. Procedures can indeed be counterproductive. If used by rote, in a mechanical way, they can create a barrier between the worker and the family, making it harder to get an accurate picture of what is going on or to develop a working relationship with the family.

There is a danger of exaggerating the importance of rules and guidelines because they are such a highly visible and politically sensitive element of child protection work. They figure largely in the set of 'performance indicators' by which local authorities are judged. The danger lies in *undervaluing* the importance and the complexity of other equally essential aspects of work that are not being measured by performance indicators. Management information systems, for instance, measure whether procedures have been followed, whether the timetable for conducting an investigation has been kept to, whether assessment forms have been completed. However, they focus mainly on measuring quantity, but it is the quality of the work that will make the difference to the child. And quality comes from the way that the worker uses the procedures, guidelines, etc., as part of the whole approach to helping the child. Procedures may specify the importance of talking to the child in an abuse investigation but it is the workers' expertise that determines whether they gain accurate, or indeed any, information from the interview or whether they help the child at all.

1.1

the purpose of sage course companions

This book aims to help students feel prepared to face the tasks and responsibilities they will be taking on. It is a short book that focuses on the knowledge base of practice, with pointers to further reading. Where relevant, it provides cross-references to the tasks or sections of statutory guidance and documents, such as the *Common Assessment Framework* (DfES, 2006a) and *Working Together to Safeguard Children* (DfES, 2006b) to help readers make the connection to their work environment.

Unlike many of the other topics in the Sage Course Companions series, child protection courses are taken as part of professional training. The goal is not just to understand a subject but to use the learning in working with families. Therefore this book does not just cover what knowledge is needed, but also the reasoning skills involved in using it. What do we know about recognising and working with abuse? Why should we respond in a particular way? What is the policy, legal and ethical framework in which we must work? And *how* do we use the knowledge base? For example, what evidence should we use? How reliable are the findings of research? How do we use evaluative studies to decide what to do to help the child?

1.2

knowing what and knowing how

Developing expertise in child protection requires far more than learning material in a book. Many of the key skills can be sketched in a textbook, but it is only through practice, experience and good supervision that they can be cultivated. Formal knowledge about child development needs to be converted into the ability to meet a child, assess the level of development and identify any areas of concern. Critical reasoning skills are honed through good reflective supervision and a supportive atmosphere that encourages workers to assess whether their picture of a family is accurate or their plan of action is well thought through.

1.3	
a note on terminology	

Child abuse investigations may be conducted with anybody in a caring role with a child but I have used the term 'parent' throughout in preference to the more impersonal word 'carer' or the more clumsy phrase 'parent or carer'. The parent is the most common focus of investigation and the term 'carer' fails to capture the unique quality of a parent–child relationship.

1.4	
who should read this book?	

This book is a course companion for anyone taking a course that includes child abuse and child protection. It is primarily aimed at social workers, but much of the material is relevant for other professionals who play a significant role in child protection. With reference to the *Common Core of Skills and Knowledge for the Children's Workforce* (DfES, 2005), this book covers material relevant to Section 3, 'Safeguarding and promoting the welfare of the child'. Many courses include some coverage of child protection: undergraduate and postgraduate social work training; postqualifying courses in social work with children and young people, their families and carers; and multi-disciplinary courses run by Local Safeguarding Children Boards. All of these courses, however, cover much more than child protection alone and so there is no precise match between the content of this book and course requirements.

1.5

benchmarks and national occupational standards

In relation to the requirements for basic social work training, it is possible to identify the key requirements to which this book will contribute. The standards for the social work degree are outcome statements that set out what a student social worker must know, understand and be able to do to be awarded the degree in social work. The National Occupational Standards for Social Work[1] set out what employers require social workers to be able to do on entering employment. The Quality Assurance Agency benchmark statement[2] for social work sets out, in outcome terms, the requirements for the achievement of an academic award at degree level. The occupational standards and the benchmark statement taken together form the basis of the assessment of students.

This book contributes in particular to achieving the following occupational standards in relation to child protection:

Key role 4: manage risk to individuals, families, carers, groups, communities, self and colleagues.

Key role 6: demonstrate professional competence in social work practice:

- research, analyse, evaluate and use current knowledge of best social work practice;
- work within agreed standards of social work practice and ensure own professional development;
- manage complex ethical issues, dilemmas and conflicts.

It also contributes to the following components of the benchmark statement:

2.4 Social work as a moral activity, requiring students to:

- recognise and work with the powerful links between intra-personal and inter-personal factors and the wider social, legal, economic, political and cultural context of people's lives;
- understand the impact of injustice, social inequalities and oppressive social relations;
- challenge constructively individual, institutional and structural discrimination;
- practise in ways that maximise safety and effectiveness in situations of uncertainty and incomplete information;
- help people to gain, regain or maintain control of their own affairs, in so far as this is compatible with their own or others' safety, well-being and rights.

2.5 The expectation that social workers will be able to act effectively in such complex circumstances requires that honours degree programmes in social work should be designed to help students learn to become accountable, reflective and self-critical. This involves learning to:

- think critically about the complex social, economic, political and cultural contexts in which social work practice is located;
- work in a transparent and responsible way, balancing autonomy with complex, multiple and sometimes contradictory accountabilities;
- exercise authority within complex frameworks of accountability and ethical and legal boundaries; and
- acquire and apply the habits of critical reflection, self-evaluation and consultation, and make appropriate use of research in the evaluation of practice outcomes.

Full details of the academic benchmarks can be obtained from the Quality Assurance Agency for Higher Education (QAA) www.qaa.org.uk.

The occupational standards are set by the strategic workforce development bodies for social care for each country. Full details can be obtained from their websites:

England: www.topss.org.uk
Northern Ireland: www.niscc.info
Scotland: www.sssc.uk.com
Wales: www.ccwales.org.uk

Students generally have the pragmatic goal of doing well enough to pass the course. However, in the case of child protection, social workers and other professionals want to achieve the highest possible standard for the sake of the children who rely on them for help. Moreover, learning does not, or at least should not, stop once the course is finished. The subject is vast and the skills are complex. There is always scope for learning in future professional practice. Continued learning is more likely to happen if the student has acquired the skills of critical, reflective practice (Kolb, 1984). Therefore this book aims to help students learn how to seek out new information, and understand how to stand back, reflect on their experience and acquire new insights into the work.

1.6

how does child abuse fit in the *Every Child Matters* agenda?

Current policy puts a strong emphasis on the importance of placing concerns about child abuse and neglect within the wider context of children's welfare in general. This is because of the way practice had become focused too narrowly on deciding whether or not the child was suffering abuse and so failed to pay attention to whether the child's general welfare and development were satisfactory (see Sections 2.1 and 2.2 for more detail). Consequently, many of the families who came to the attention of the child protection system were found not to be abusive and the case was closed, despite there being clear evidence that, for other reasons, the child's needs were not being fully met (Department of Health, 1995).

The current *Every Child Matters* agenda is concerned about helping *all* children in the UK fulfil their potential and safeguarding them from all sources of adversity. Child abuse and neglect are only two of the possible causes of poor outcomes for children and only in some cases will they be severe enough to meet the criteria of causing or being at risk of causing significant harm. It is important not to treat abuse and neglect in isolation but to look at the child's and the family's wider needs. Working with cases involving abuse and neglect draws on the general skills and knowledge of working with children and parents. Knowledge of what non-abusive families behave like is crucial in identifying abusive families. However, there is a substantive body of knowledge and skills about abuse and neglect – of what abusive families look like and how to work with them – and these are the subject of this book. *Although child abuse concerns can be described as another form of need – a need for protection – it will be a recurrent theme in this book that dealing with abuse and neglect also draws on a distinct set of knowledge, skills and values.*

1.7	
when does imperfect parenting become abusive?	

Abusive/neglectful behaviour has to be seen as part of a continuum of parenting behaviour, ranging from the excellent to the murderous. The 'perfect' parent is an ideal; Winnicot's (1951) concept of the 'good enough' parent offers a more realistic and achievable standard for parents to aspire to. Views on 'good enough' parenting vary over time and between cultures. Even within one culture at a specific time, families vary a great deal, at the micro level, in how they express affection, administer discipline or deal with anger. There can be major difficulties, in practice, in agreeing on the boundary between what is acceptable and what is unacceptable.

> *When Parliament was debating the Children Act 2004, there were heated debates about whether any level of physical chastisement was acceptable or whether all forms should be considered abusive and made illegal. The final decision was to continue to allow 'reasonable' physical punishment by those with parental responsibility but that this did not authorise actions serious enough to be considered assault.*

However, although there are difficulties in deciding exactly where to draw lines between abusive/poor/acceptable parenting behaviour, they are still meaningful categories. In many cases, the classification is quite straightforward. The MPs who disagreed about hitting children were in complete agreement that it was abusive to hit a child so hard that bones were broken. It is at the boundaries that problems in classification occur, resulting in serious difficulties in practice because the decision on how to view the parent's behaviour leads to significantly different responses from the professionals. This issue recurs at several points in this book.

1.8

how to use the book

This book contains two further Parts – Two and Three – that complement and support one another and, if used together, should help you become more informed and competent as a student.

Part Two covers the core areas of the curriculum. It begins with a brief overview of the running themes of child abuse work, themes that run throughout work with families and shape the way policy and knowledge is applied in practice. These running themes will be mentioned again and amplified throughout later sections. Sections 2.1–2.3 cover the contextual background: the history of society's reaction to child abuse, the current policy, and the current legal framework. Sections 2.4–2.5 deal with issues relating to the knowledge base, by, firstly, examining the difficulty of working with the uncertainty that is inherent in child protection work and, secondly, discussing how to find and use research to develop your understanding. Sections 2.6–2.11 deal with the knowledge base, looking at problems in defining abuse and neglect and the theories of why they happen, before devoting a section to each of the four categories of abuse and neglect. Section 2.12 reviews what can be done to make children safer. Each section contains key references and suggestions on taking the subject further.

Part Three of this book has been designed to help you develop and sharpen the study skills that are necessary for studying child protection and for practising as a child protection professional. It is intended to help you improve your study, writing and revision skills, and should be combined with the academic knowledge in Part Two. The aim is for Parts Two and Three to support each other and be used together.

The final section, Part Four, provides a glossary, a section on the Scottish legal framework, and References.

A final feature of the book is the inclusion of 'Tips' throughout. These are intended to highlight areas for you to consider, or to remind you of how this section links to earlier reading. The Tips include some practical advice, or alert you to issues about which mistakes or misunderstanding often occur in practice.

Notes

1 This is based on the most recent document available at the time of publication: TOPSS UK Partnership (2002) *National Occupational Standards for Social Workers*. Leeds: TOPSS.
2 This is based on the most recent document available at the time of publication: QAA (2000) *Social Policy Administration and Social Work Benchmark Statement*. Gloucester: QAA.

part two

core areas of the curriculum

running themes in child protection work

The primary focus of this book is on the formal knowledge base of child protection work: the policy and legal context, and the theories and research on the causes, consequences and intervention options of abuse and neglect. In working with families, this material has to be integrated with the values and skills that are equally essential elements of good practice. The running themes in this book are reminders of the key people and values involved in practice; places where they are particularly relevant will be highlighted in later chapters.

Running themes

Throughout the child protection process, it is important to try to remember these running themes and think about how they may be relevant to your work.

- **The voice of the child**   The prime focus of child protection work is the safety and welfare of the child and it is essential to remember to treat the child as a human being with rights and not as an object of concern.
- **Working with parents**   How should they be treated – as partners or suspects? How can their role as partners with professionals be maximised while investigating them for abuse or neglect?
- **Working with other professionals**   The child protection system operates on a multi-disciplinary basis. What is the role of other professionals in a particular case? How should they be involved?
- **Values/professional code of ethics**   There is a moral dimension to all work with human beings that limits the way they can be treated. For social care workers, the moral principles of their work are included in the General Social Care Council's code of practice (available at www.gscc.org.uk). Child protection work raises particular complexities relating to balancing the rights and needs of the child and the parents, and of using coercion in working with families.
- **Anti-discriminatory practice**   It is important to ensure that people are not adversely assessed or treated because of their race, ethnicity, religion, gender or disability. Child protection work raises two particular areas of concern: misinterpreting unfamiliar cultural practices as abnormal or harmful, and adversely judging a parent because of prejudices.

- **Emotional impact**   Child protection work has a significant emotional impact, both on family members and on the professionals involved. Failure to acknowledge and deal with emotions constructively has an adverse impact on the quality of the work and on the well-being of the family and the professional.

2.1

the history of child abuse

Learning outcomes

This section will help you to understand:

- The key factors influencing family life.
- How society's concern for child abuse has developed in the past 100 years.
- How attempts have been made at several times to develop preventive services but with limited success.
- The key events that have shaped public attitudes and professional responses to child abuse.
- How the UK system compares with those of other countries.

Current policy and practice needs to be understood in its wider social and historical context. The two main areas to consider are:

1 The general context of family life.

2 The history of society's response to child abuse.

The general context of family life

The nature of childhood

In today's society, children have a long period of dependency on adults during which they are, to varying degrees, protected from full adult responsibilities. In the past, children were seen as having special needs for only a very short time in infancy. Thereafter, they played their part in family life and work in line with their abilities.

Challenges to the patriarchal family

The patriarchal family was the dominant form for many centuries, with fathers being given considerable authority to make decisions on behalf of women and children. The changing role of women in recent decades and their increased economic power has radically altered this model.

Child rights

The United Nations Convention on the Rights of the Child (1989) has been ratified by all countries except the USA and Somalia. The UK ratification of this convention illustrates the changing view of the 'child as property' to the 'child as an individual with rights'.

Violence in the family

In the patriarchal family system, violence towards wives and children was seen as mainly a private matter, and even in the latter half of the twentieth century police were reluctant to get involved in violence within a marriage, classing incidents as 'just a domestic'. As women and children have become seen as individuals with rights, their right to safety from violence has also been recognised (Parton, 2005: 58).

Changing family structures

Divorce and births outside marriage have both become more common in recent decades so that many more children are not living with both birth parents. Lone-parent households increased from 2 per cent to 7 per cent of all households between 1961 and 1999 (Ferri, Bynner and Wadsworth, 2003).

Economic conditions

In the early 1900s, training for NSPCC officers included information on how to deal with a dead body, since there was a real possibility of finding one when making a home visit. Due to extreme poverty, poor sanitation and infectious diseases, a third of children in poor areas did not reach their first birthday. Rising affluence has meant that such extreme poverty is now rare but many children do live in relative poverty. In government policy documents on 'children in need', children living in poverty are classified as 'vulnerable' and currently number around 3 million.

Social exclusion

Nowadays, it is not just the economic condition of poverty that is seen to have an adverse effect on children's development but the associated conditions of being unable to participate fully in social life. Government policies to tackle poverty are therefore linked to policies to improve housing, educational achievement and community strengths.

The history of society's response to child abuse

Milestones in the history of child abuse

Recognition of child abuse involves not just acceptance that it occurs but that it is wrong.

Late nineteeth century

Growing public concern about the conditions in which children were living in industrialised towns and condemnation of parental violence led to the formation of the National Society for the Prevention of Cruelty to Children (NSPCC) in 1887. This was modelled on the American Society for the Prevention of Cruelty to Children, formed after the first successful prosecution for child abuse in 1874. That prosecution had been brought under legislation against cruelty to animals.

A church social worker found that 8-year-old Mary Ellen Wilson was being repeatedly beaten and starved by her stepmother. The social worker could find no one willing to interfere in family life and so, in desperation, she went to the Society for the Prevention of Cruelty to Animals. She argued that a human child was an animal and so covered by the law against cruelty to animals. The stepmother was successfully prosecuted under this law.

1889 Prevention of Cruelty to and Protection of Children Act

This put a limit on how violent a father could be but still allowed considerable scope for physical chastisement.

Running theme: the voice of the child

Historically, the voice of the child was not heard – it is only recently that the importance of the child's opinion and evidence has been recognised. The class difference between many parents and professionals has meant that parents, too, have traditionally been given little power in the working relationship.

1908 Incest Act

Sex abuse in the form of incest between father and daughter was recognised and outlawed by this legislation. However, few prosecutions were brought (24 cases in its first year).

1948 Children Act

This legislation set up child care departments in local authorities and created the social work role of 'child care officer'. It was a part of the post-war creation of a welfare state and embodied a belief that the state should take a positive and supportive approach to the family to ensure children were given the appropriate conditions in which to develop (Parton, 1991: 21). It marked the beginnings of contemporary debates about the importance of preventive work to support families (Hardiker, Exton and Barker, 1991: 12) but it gave local authorities very limited power to develop preventive services.

1963 Children and Young Persons Act

Section 1 broadened the preventive remit of local authorities, authorising them to:

> Make available such advice, guidance and assistance as may promote the welfare of children by diminishing the need to receive children into or keep them in care ... or to bring children before a juvenile court. (Children and Young Persons Act, 1963, section 1)
>
> The provision of speedy and effective help, once early difficulties had been identified, was intended to head off the greater difficulties that would eventually contribute to the break up of the family. (Hardiker, Exton and Barker, 1991: 13)

Preventing juvenile delinquency was a greater concern than preventing other childhood problems. Again, the impact of this preventive policy was muted by resource restrictions.

1968 Seebohm Report

The inquiry into welfare services in England and Wales chaired by Lord Seebohm led to the creation of social services departments in 1972, integrating the separate strands of social work into one profession. The aim was to provide a unified service to families. The report also concluded that welfare services needed to widen their preventive remit even further: they should 'undertake work other than that caused by families and individuals in the late or final stages of dependence, disintegration and despair' (Seebohm Committee, 1968: para. 454). The Kilbrandon Report in Scotland led to a major reorganisation of services into social work departments.

1960s

The recent concern for child abuse is usually dated to the pioneering work of Henry Kempe, an American paediatrician who produced X-ray evidence for the existence of repeated physical abuse of young children by a parent or carer. His seminal article in 1962 and his determined efforts to publicise the dangers facing children raised public awareness and concern. He conceptualised child abuse as a medical problem requiring diagnosis by doctors, calling it 'the battered baby syndrome' and thereby disassociating it from concepts of poverty or deprivation. His work was disseminated in the UK in the 1960s but it was the tragic death of a child in the UK that triggered wider public appreciation of the problem.

1974 The inquiry report into the death of Maria Colwell

Maria Colwell was a little girl of 7-years-old who was killed by her stepfather after months of physical and emotional abuse and neglect. Because the death was so shocking there was a public inquiry into the care she had received from professionals. She had been removed from her mother by social workers at a few months old because she was being badly cared for, and spent most of her life living with an aunt under the supervision of the social workers. Her mother had remarried and had four more children and then asked to have Maria home again. Social workers thought it would be in Maria's best interests to be with her birth mother so, against Maria's wishes,

> *she was returned. The next few months before her death were terrible. She*
> *was treated as a servant, not a daughter, and made to do many heavy tasks*
> *such as collecting large sacks of coal. She was also poorly fed and lost*
> *weight. She was severely beaten on several occasions, before finally dying*
> *from her injuries.*

The public inquiry (DHSS 1974) found that many people had known some of the misery Maria was enduring and many had tried to get help for her but had been unsuccessful because no one had put all the information together to appreciate fully what danger she was in. The overall picture was of numerous well-intentioned people each with a partial picture that underestimated the severity of the abuse she was suffering. The inquiry did not blame individuals but concluded that 'it was the "system", using the word in its widest sense, which failed her' (DHSS, 1974: 86). The lesson that was drawn was the need to improve training to recognise the signs and symptoms of child abuse and to set up mechanisms to facilitate the sharing of information to get a more accurate assessment of what was happening to a child. The recommendations of this inquiry produced the basic structure of today's child protection system, with an emphasis on professional collaboration and the use of case conferences as a means of reaching a shared assessment.

1985   The inquiry report into the death of Jasmine Beckford

After 1974, a steady stream of public inquiries into child deaths had led to child abuse being increasingly prioritised and the procedures for professionals working together gradually formalised. However, another significant impetus to the development of the child protection system came in 1985 with the report into the death of Jasmine Beckford. Her story echoed that of Maria Colwell to an uncanny extent and made the public question whether professionals were making any progress in tackling child abuse.

> *Like Maria, Jasmine had been removed from her birth family because of con-*
> *cerns about abuse, but later returned under social work supervision. Again,*
> *the social worker had failed to recognise the signs of abuse and mistakenly*
> *thought Jasmine was safe.*

The public inquiry (London Borough of Brent, 1985), chaired by Louis Blom-Cooper, was scathing in its criticisms of the professionals involved, particularly of the social workers who were castigated for putting the needs of the parents above those of the child and failing to recognise the significance of signs of abuse. It urged social workers to remember their statutory responsibilities to the child and led to an increasingly legalistic approach to child protection (Parton, 2005: 54).

1988   The Cleveland inquiry

In contrast to earlier inquiries which had examined professionals' failure to protect a child, this one looked at a series of cases where it seemed that professionals had been acting too quickly in removing children from their parents and raised questions about the balance of power between parents and the state. In a few weeks in 1987, over 100 children were removed from their families on emergency Place of Safety Orders on the basis of a diagnosis of sexual abuse made by two paediatricians at a hospital in Middlesbrough. The resulting outcry by the families aroused media and political attention that led to the establishment of a public inquiry to examine the basis of the decisions to remove the children.

This first inquiry into alleged *over-reaction* by professionals instead of under-reaction had a number of unusual features. It was concerned with sexual abuse, which had not received a great deal of public attention until then. It affected middle-class families, not just the poor or the marginalised. It also directed criticism at the medical profession as much as at social work. The message from the inquiry was that professionals needed to take a more legalistic approach to collecting evidence, with an emphasis on collecting evidence that could be used in court.

1989   The Children Act

The aim of the Act was to set a new balance between the state and the family, increasing the protection of the family from untoward state interference. It encouraged an approach to child welfare based on negotiation, involving parents and children in agreed plans as far as possible. Although the word 'partnership' was not in the Act itself, it was a key principle in the accompanying guidance. The Act also encouraged provision of family support at an early stage of difficulty to reduce the need for more coercive interventions later. The concept of 'prevention' was broadened from a simple duty to prevent children coming into care to include a broad power to provide services to promote the care and upbringing of children within their families.

1992   The Orkney inquiry

In the early 1990s, there were a number of cases involving organised and institutional (residential homes and nurseries) abuse where the focus was not on behaviour within the family but outside it. The most prominent was an incident in Orkney in which nine children from four families were taken into care and removed to the mainland following allegations of organised sexual abuse. After five weeks in care, a court hearing judged the proceedings were incompetent and dismissed the cases, leading to the children's return home. The media coverage portrayed reasonable, caring parents fighting against injustice, contrasted with interfering, intolerant social workers. The inquiry led to the establishment of procedures for dealing with such allegations of organised abuse.

1995   Messages from Research

The Department of Health published a set of large studies on the functioning of the child welfare system, summarised in the book *Messages from Research*. They revealed that the cumulative effect of adverse publicity and policy changes had been that professionals, especially social workers, were prioritising child abuse concerns over other types of referral. Moreover, a fear of missing a case had led to the lowering of the threshold for triggering an investigation into abuse so that the number of investigations being done had increased markedly, reducing the time and resources for dealing with other aspects of child need. Another criticism of the system was that the majority of cases investigated were not substantiated and the families then usually received no further service despite often being in circumstances where they were struggling to cope.

The sharp division between child protection and child in need cases was seen as problematic, leading to an emphasis on assessing the immediate risks to the child and not the wider social and psychological needs. Policy therefore urged a 're-focusing' of child protection in the context of children in need looking at all the child's needs, not just their need for protection from abuse.

Remember how painful it is for families to be investigated – to accuse a parent or their partner of abuse or neglect is a major charge. Whether guilty or innocent, the emotional impact is considerable and can lead to a variety of responses – anxiety, fear, distress, anger, denial. Research has revealed how traumatic the experience of being investigated is for many families (Bell, 1999; Thoburn, Lewis and Shemmings, 1995). It is inevitable that the process of an investigation is painful and intrusive to some degree, however sensitively handled, but professionals need to remain aware of the impact they are having on the family and try to minimise it. A moving personal account of the experience of being investigated has been written by Richardson (2003).

2000   The death of Victoria Climbie

Victoria's death shocked the public because, despite being seen by numerous professionals during the preceding months, none had accurately seen the abuse she was enduring. She was 8-years-old when she died from hypothermia, and the post-mortem found 128 separate injuries on her body as a result of having been beaten with a range of sharp and blunt instruments. She was born in the Ivory Coast but had moved to London 11 months earlier, after a short stay in Paris. In London, she was known to four social services departments, three housing authorities, two police child protection teams, two hospitals and an NSPCC family centre. The findings of the public inquiry corroborated government thinking about the need to fundamentally restructure children's services so that child protection issues did not dominate to the exclusion of meeting other and lower-level needs of children.

Running theme: the voice of the child

Practice guidance stresses the importance of talking to the child but this is often not done. In Victoria's case, despite so many professionals being involved, *no one* had a meaningful conversation with her in the eight months she was known to public agencies (Laming, 2003). Research shows that, all too often, children are not fully recognised as active participants either as a source of knowledge about what is happening in the family or as a source of opinions about what should be done (Gough, 1997).

2003   Every Child Matters Green Paper

This sets out the current policy that is discussed in detail in the next section. The government wants to transform the culture of children's services from a mainly reactive, crisis-led service dealing predominantly with child protection cases to one in which all children's needs are recognised and responded to at an early stage. 'Early intervention' and 'prevention' are the key concepts. Echoing previous preventive policies, the expectation is that if children's and parents' needs are identified and met at an early stage, there will be a reduction in the number of families who go on to develop serious problems, including abuse or neglect.

2004   The Children Act

This latest legislation creates a Children's Commissioner and prescribes organisational restructuring and information-processing systems to encourage professional collaboration and increased collection and sharing of data about children to help professionals identify needs at an early stage and then provide help to meet those needs.

Comparison with other countries

Realising how differently some other countries conceptualise and respond to child abuse helps us to understand how culturally specific the UK development of policy and practice has been. The political scientist Esping-Anderson (1990) has grouped industrialised countries into three main types: Anglo-American, Continental European and Scandinavian. They have different legal and welfare traditions that lead to significantly different types of support for families in general and this, in turn, leads to different forms of child protection systems.

The Anglo-American group consists of the UK and its former colonies – the USA, Canada, Australia and New Zealand. They have a mainly market-oriented welfare system, with relatively meagre, means-tested state benefits for the residual poor. There tends to be a high level of stigmatisation because benefits are seen as disincentives to work. Social solidarity tends not to be a high priority. Within this system, there are minimal universal services to support families, with a strong emphasis on selective help. In relation to child protection, the selection criteria are related to the severity of the problems rather than to money. The high value given to the autonomy of the family means that, in child protection, there is an emphasis on legal justification for interfering in family life, contributing to a confrontational approach.

The Continental European group – France, Germany, Italy, Austria, for example – have a stronger benefit system but most benefits are linked to employment. The principle of subsidiarity is important, encouraging the devolution of provision to the lowest possible level so that it is the local community rather than the state that delivers services. The legal system for child protection facilitates a less confrontational approach than in the UK. In Germany, for example, social workers are concerned to earn the trust of the family because their voluntary engagement is seen as pivotal (Hetherington, 2002: 26).

The Scandinavian group have stronger universal benefits. It favours universal and equalising provision, with a strong belief in social solidarity. It provides more family services than other regimes.

Comparison with other countries draws attention to the way that the UK's division between family support and child protection flows from the liberal welfare regime in which it operates. The importance of the cultural context in which policy is made raises questions about the feasibility of integrating support and protection as is envisaged by the *Every Child Matters* agenda: 'There is a contradiction between discouraging reliance on state support and encouraging more supportive interventions with families' (Hetherington, 2002: 30).

Taking it *FURTHER*

Is there still a tendency to treat children as property despite the impact of the rights movement? When the government talks of the importance of investing in children because they are '100 per cent of our future', does this imply some sense of ownership, albeit by the state rather than the parents? What are the alternatives to a child being regarded as property? What reasons other than investing in the country's future could be given for meeting the basic needs of children? What is the justification for considering parents have a unique relationship with their children that gives them a special claim to judge what is in their best interests? Are there any problems with the state deciding what children need?

Further Reading

R. HETHERINGTON, A. COOPER, P. SMITH AND G. WILFORD (1997) *Protecting Children: messages from Europe. Lyme Regis: Russell House Publishing. This key text gives a detailed and fascinating comparison of several European countries, illustrating how much range there is in the power given to children to have a say in what happens to them, in the nature of the relationship between suspected and proven abusers and professionals, and the availability of support for families under stress.*

On the nature of childhood:

P. ARIES (1962) *Centuries of Childhood, London: Jonathan Cape. A classic text on the subject, much quoted.*

L. DE MAUSE (ED.) (1976) *The History of Childhood, London: Souvenir Press.*

A. JAMES AND A. PROUT (EDS) (1997) *Constructing and Re-constructing Childhood, London: Falmer Press.*

L. POLLOCK (1983) *Forgotten Children: parent–child relations from 1500 to 1900, Cambridge: Cambridge University Press.*

On the nature of child protection work:

H. FERGUSON (2004) *Protecting Children in Time: child abuse, child protection and the consequences of modernity, Basingstoke: Palgrave Macmillan.*

N. PARTON (1985) *The Politics of Child Abuse, Basingstoke: Macmillan.*

N. PARTON (2005) *Safeguarding Children: early intervention and surveillance in a late modern society, Basingstoke: Palgrave Macmillan.*

Empirical research on how services are operating:

B. CORBY (1987) *Working with Child Abuse, Milton Keynes: Open University Press.*

DEPARTMENT OF HEALTH (1995) *Messages from Research, London: The Stationery Office. Provides brief summaries of twenty empirical studies and the revisions to government policy that they have triggered.*

E. FARMER AND M. OWEN (1995) *Child Protection Practice: private risks and public remedies – decision making, intervention and outcome in child protection, London: HMSO. One of the key studies in the influential set published in 1995, illustrating the negative experience so many families have when investigated by the child protection system.*

J. GIBBONS, S. CONROY AND C. BELL (1995) *Operating the Child Protection System: a study of child protection practices in English local authorities, London: HMSO. Another seminal study that showed how many child protection investigations led to no useful service for the child.*

2.2	
current policy	

Learning outcomes

This section will help you understand:

- The scope of the government's policies for safeguarding children.
- That the responsibility for safeguarding children is shared by all agencies working with children.
- Where child protection concerns fit within the wider safeguarding agenda.

The safeguarding agenda

The new approach to children's policy, embodied in *Every Child Matters: change for children* (Treasury, 2003) requires a radical transformation of both the organisation and the culture of practice from a reactive service for a few to a proactive one where all children's needs are identified and met at a low level of concern, instead of waiting for some of them to escalate into serious problems. As this chapter will detail, it involves change at every level of all services for children (not just social services) and will take several years to implement. Many of the innovative ideas such as a Common Assessment Framework and the Integrated Children's Service are being piloted and will be modified in the light of experience. Therefore, at this stage, it is impossible to provide a conclusive account of policy, since developments and amendments are continually being published. Readers are therefore warned that there may have been significant new developments in policy and practice by the time they are reading this section, and there may be important omissions. Fortunately, the government website, www.everychildmatters.gov.uk, provides up-to-date information on the major policy innovations and readers are advised to consult it.

There will also be some degree of variation at the local level on how the national policies are implemented so that practitioners will need to learn their local organisational structure and procedures.

The Green Paper *Every Child Matters* (Treasury, 2003) is the key document, setting out the government's proposals and its policy of developing preventive and supportive services:

> We need to shift away from associating parent support with crisis interventions to a more consistent offer of parenting support throughout a child's and young person's life. We will work towards a mix of universal and targeted parenting approaches, including advice and information, home visiting and parenting classes. (para. 3.6)

The Prime Minister, Tony Blair, summed up the political drive behind the policy in his introduction to the Green Paper:

> This country is still one where life chances are unequal. This damages not only those children born into disadvantages, but our society as a whole. We all stand to share the benefits of an economy and society with less educational failure, higher skills, less crime, and better health. We all share a duty to do everything we can to ensure every child has the chance to fulfil their potential.

The four key themes of the paper were summarised as:

1 Increasing the focus on supporting families and carers – the most critical influence on children's lives.

2 Ensuring necessary intervention takes place before children reach crisis point and protecting children from falling through the net.

3 Addressing the underlying problems identified in the report into the death of Victoria Climbie – weak accountability and poor integration.

4 Ensuring that the people working with children are valued, rewarded and trained. (www.everychildmatters.gov.uk/aims/background; accessed 6 December 2005)

The scope of children's services has been dramatically widened. The government's aim is for every child, whatever their background or their circumstances, to have the support they need to:

- be healthy
- stay safe
- enjoy and achieve
- make a positive contribution
- achieve economic well-being.

Additional clarification of what is meant by these somewhat abstract goals is then given in the table opposite.

Key government publications setting out *Every Child Matters* policy and practice:

1 *Working Together to Safeguard Children* (DFES 2006b) is the key official document setting out the new arrangements for inter-agency co-operation in relation to both safeguarding from all adverse effects and, more specifically, responding to a concern that a child might be at risk of significant harm.

2 *The Common Assessment Framework*: sets out a framework to be used by all in children's services to improve shared understanding and co-operation. It includes guidance on information-sharing within and between agencies, and organisational boundaries.

Overall outcome	Includes...
Stay safe	Safe from maltreatment, neglect, violence and sexual exploitation
	Safe from accidental injury and death
	Safe from bullying and discrimination
	Safe from crime and anti-social behaviour in and out of school
	Have security, stability and are cared for
Be healthy	Physically healthy
	Mentally and emotionally healthy
	Sexually healthy
	Healthy lifestyles
	Choose not to take illegal drugs
Enjoy and achieve	Ready for school
	Attend and enjoy school
	Achieve stretching national educational standards at primary school
	Achieve personal and social development and enjoy recreation
	Achieve stretching national educational standards at secondary school
Make a positive contribution	Engage in decision making and support the community and environment
	Engage in law-abiding and positive behaviour in and out of school
	Develop positive relationships and choose not to bully or discriminate
	Develop self-confidence and successfully deal with significant life changes and challenges
	Develop enterprising behaviour
Achieve economic well-being	Engage in further education, employment or training on leaving school
	Ready for employment
	Live in decent homes and sustainable communities
	Access to transport and material goods
	Live in households free from low income

3 *The Common Core of Skills and Knowledge* (DfES, 2005); linked to the *Children's Workforce Strategy*, sets out a curriculum that should be covered by all working in children's services, again with the aim of improving shared understanding and co-operation.

4 *Lead Professional Good Practice Guidance*: sets out the key responsibilities, skills and knowledge required by practitioners to carry out this function.

There are several strong arguments for providing a more comprehensive service to children and families:

Economic: the Prime Minister, in the quote above, highlighted the economic argument for helping all children fulfil their potential by offering help with any needs/problems they display. It will lead to a better educated, healthier, and, one hopes, happier set of adults who will be more economically productive.

Moral: since the UK has ratified the United Nations Convention on the Rights of the Child, it has also accepted a moral responsibility to meet children's rights to having their basic needs met.

Pragmatic: there is a pragmatic argument for offering help with minor and moderate problems: some of them will escalate into major problems – of delinquency, serious mental illness, educational failure, etc. These are much worse for the child to experience, harder to deal with, and a heavy drain on services. The ideal would be to target early intervention services on those children who are likely to go on to develop serious troubles. However, we lack the knowledge to identify this group of children accurately at an early stage. Therefore, services need to be provided on a wider scale so that they catch the children for whom the minor and moderate problems might turn out to be 'early warnings' of major problems to come.

Where child protection fits in the safeguarding agenda

Safeguarding is defined as:

- protecting children from maltreatment;
- preventing impairment of children's health and development;
- ensuring that children are growing up in circumstances consistent with the provision of safe and effective care; and
- undertaking that role so as to enable those children to have optimum life chances and to enter adulthood successfully. (*Working Together* to *Safeguard Children*, DfES, 2006: 5)

Child protection is defined as: 'a part of safeguarding and promoting welfare. This refers to the activity which is undertaken to protect specific children who are suffering or are at risk of suffering significant harm' (ibid.: 5).

All children's services share the responsibility for safeguarding children. Whatever the specific focus of their contact – education, health, etc. – they have a duty to have regard to the child's overall health and development. If they identify a need or a cause for concern, they should take action to deal with it. There are four main responses for any professional who has a concern that a child has 'additional needs', defined as those who need targeted or specialist support to progress towards the five priority outcomes to: be healthy, stay safe, enjoy and achieve, make a positive contribution, and achieve economic well-being.

> *Response 1*: the help needed may be easily assessed and arranged, for example it may be evident that an in-depth single-agency response is needed, such as speech therapy, and a direct referral is made.
> *Response 2*: completing a Common Assessment Framework. This may be undertaken by any of a range of professionals and forms the basis for deciding what other services, if any, are needed, and provides more evidence-based referrals to targeted or specialist agencies. Local procedures give guidance on when to undertake a CAF.
> *Response 3*: referral to a local authority as a 'child in need' under Section 17 of the Children Act 1989. The social worker and manager will decide, within 24 hours, whether socal care involvement is appropriate and, if so, carry out an initial assessment within seven days.
> *Response 4*: referral to a local authority as a child in need of protection, possibly requiring a Section 47 inquiry. Again, the social worker and manager will decide how to respond. If a Section 47 inquiry is undertaken, then there are detailed procedures and a timetable set out in the local procedure manual.

If there is concern about the child's immediate safety at any time, then emergency action should be taken to safeguard the child. Also, if any concerns about significant harm arise at any point, this will trigger a move to a Section 47 inquiry.

The threshold for 'significant harm'

In practice, professionals face complex problems in deciding both whether the child's needs are related to parental abuse or neglect and whether they are experiencing, or are at risk of experiencing, significant harm. As the previous section on the history of child protection showed, errors in assessing a child as the victim of abuse and errors in judging the severity of the danger they are in have provoked vocal criticisms of professionals from the media and the public. This has contributed to the defensive practice which led to the skewed dominance of child protection investigations to the detriment of other services for children – the state of affairs the safeguarding agenda aims to change.

Working Together to Safeguard Children gives guidance on judging 'significant harm'.

> 1.24 There are no absolute criteria on which to rely when judging what constitutes significant harm. Consideration of the severity of the ill-treatment may include the degree and the extent of physical harm, the duration and frequency of abuse and neglect, and the extent of premeditation, degree of threat and coercion, sadism, and bizarre or unusual elements in child sexual abuse. … Sometimes, a single traumatic event may constitute significant harm e.g. a violent assault, suffocation or poisoning. More often, significant harm is a compilation of significant events, both acute and longstanding, which interrupt, change or damage the child's physical and psychological development.

Further guidance is given in para. 1.25 on the factors to consider:

- the nature of harm, in terms of maltreatment or failure to provide adequate care;
- the impact on the child's health and development;
- the child's development within the context of their family and wider environment;
- any special needs, such as a medical condition, communication impairment or disability that may affect the child's development and care within the family;
- the capacity of the parents to meet adequately the child's needs; and
- the wider and environmental family context.

Working Together acknowledges the unavoidable element of uncertainty in making these decisions:

> 1.13 Children have varying needs which change over time. Judgements on how best to intervene when there are concerns about harm to a child will often and unavoidably entail an element of risk – at the extreme, of leaving a child for too long in a dangerous situation or of removing a child unnecessarily from their family. The way to proceed in the face of uncertainty is through competent professional judgements based on a sound assessment of the child's needs, the parents' capacity to respond to those needs – including their capacity to keep the child safe from significant harm – and the wider family circumstances.

Section 17 and Section 47 thresholds

In practice, the decision on whether to classify a referral as a Section 17 or Section 47 is very challenging. The small amount of information contained in a referral may be open to different interpretations and the more accurate interpretation only becomes clear when the family has been more thoroughly assessed. In some child death inquiries, failure to protect the child has been traced back to faulty decision making about the nature of the referral. The inquiry into the death of Victoria Climbie, for example, noted how the early social work assessment that she did not require a Section 47 inquiry led to all future information being misinterpreted in a less worrying light, so that the degree of abuse she was enduring was not seen.

Thorpe and Bilson (1998) offer helpful criteria to differentiate the two levels of concern:

Section 47

1. Information has been offered that clearly indicates a child has been harmed or injured, or an adult has behaved in a way that would normally cause harm or injury, and an investigation is needed to clarify this information.
2. It is necessary to clarify whether the alleged actions were deliberately intended to cause harm or injury or were the consequence of an accident or excessive discipline.
3. It is necessary to investigate if allegations have been received from a number of different sources.
4. It is necessary to determine if reports are required from other professionals in health, education and criminal justice who have first-hand evidence of the alleged harm or injury.

Section 17

1. Parents are having difficulties and support is required to help look after children.
2. An assessment is needed to clarify the type of support required and which agency is most appropriate to deliver this support.
3. The moral character of parents is given as reason for concern over care of the children.
4. General concerns are expressed about care of the children but no direct allegation of harm is made.

Dealing with a child protection referral

Once a child protection referral to a social care team has been made, there is detailed guidance on how to proceed, set out in *Working Together to Safeguard Children,* and in local guidance.

The Integrated Children's System that is being introduced is an electronic case management system for social care workers. The ICS will include several forms to document the progress in dealing with a referral. The key ones for children in need (including children in need of protection), in order of use, are:

Contact record
Referral and Information Record (completed within 1 working day)
Initial Assessment, which includes Initial Plan (completed within 7 working days)
Core Assessment Record (completed within 35 working days)
Child's Plan which includes Child Protection Plan
Record of Strategy Discussion
Record of S47 Inquiries which includes Initial Plan
Initial Child Protection Conference Report, which includes Outline Child Protection Plan
Chronology
Review Records
Closure Record

Running theme: the voice of the child

Practice is being increasingly structured by procedures and timetables. These are primarily designed around adult competences and can be ill-matched to the needs of children for time, flexibility and creativity in helping them communicate and participate in the child protection process. Bell's (2002) qualitative study of children involved in a child protection investigation concluded that children can best be helped to participate through the development and maintenance of a relationship of trust, offered by a key professional in their network.

Confidentiality

The usual rules of confidentiality do not apply when you are concerned that a child is suffering or at risk of suffering significant harm. Government guidance lists six key principles on sharing information (HM Government, 2006: 5).

• You should explain to children, young people and families at the outset, openly and honestly, what and how information will, or could be shared and why, and seek their agreement. The exception to this is where to do so would put that child, young person or others at increased risk of significant harm or an adult at risk of serious harm, or if it would undermine the prevention, detection or prosecution of a serious crime (see Glossary for definition), including where seeking consent might lead to interference with any potential investigation.

- You must always consider the safety and welfare of a child or young person when making decisions on whether to share information about them. Where there is concern that the child may be suffering or is at risk of suffering significant harm, the child's safety and welfare must be the overriding consideration.
- You should, where possible, respect the wishes of children, young people or families who do not consent to share confidential information. You may still share information if, in your judgement on the facts of the case, there is sufficient need to override that lack of consent.
- You should seek advice where you are in doubt, especially where your doubt relates to a concern about possible significant harm to a child or serious harm to others.
- You should ensure that the information you share is accurate and up-to date, necessary for the purpose for which you are sharing it, shared only with those people who need to see it, and shared securely.
- You should always record the reasons for your decision – whether it is to share information or not.

Taking it *FURTHER*

Does shifting the focus from reactive to preventive services carry any risks? Is there a danger that child protection concerns will receive less attention as professionals are focused on working in partnership with parents to support them and so are slow to be suspicious of abuse or neglect? Conversely, might the powerful social drives that made child protection so dominant still be operating so that, in practice, little changes?

Further Reading

B. FAWCETT, B. FEATHERSTONE AND J. GODDARD (2004) *Contemporary Child Care Policy and Practice, Basingstoke: Palgrave Macmillan. Places current developments in their historical context and offers a good critique of how the system has become polarised between child protection and family support. Raises concerns about how the new emphasis on safeguarding children may negatively impact on child protection.*

N. PARTON (2005) *Safeguarding Childhood: early intervention and surveillance in a late modern society, Basingstoke: Palgrave Macmillan. Provides a detailed analysis of how policy has changed, stressing the increased importance given to regulation and surveillance of family life as a means of preventing problems.*

THE TREASURY (2003) *Every Child Matters: Change for children. London: HMSO. This is the Green Paper that sets out the government's vision for children's services.*

2.3 the legal framework	

Learning outcomes

This section will help you to understand:

* The key sections of legislation that are most used in child protection work.

* The principles underlying the legislation in relation to children.

* The key features of procedures for dealing with concerns about child abuse and neglect.

There are a large number of laws that have some relevance to work with children and families but this chapter looks specifically at the legislation of closest relevance to dealing with cases of abuse and neglect. Child protection work is guided by:

The legal framework for practice, setting out duties and powers. The key legislation is the Children Act 1989, modified by the Children Act 2004.

Central government guidance, the key document being *Working Together to Safeguard Children 2006*, published by the Department for Education and Skills.

Local guidance, detailing local procedures, key personnel and how to contact them, the sequence of what to do, and time-scales for carrying out the inquiry. Previously developed by the local Area Child Protection Committees, they now come under the remit of their replacements: the Local Safeguarding Children Boards (LSCB).

The law gives social workers and the other caring professions their mandate to practise. It sets out not only the duties but also the powers of the various agencies in providing help and protection to children. The legislation differs between the four countries in the United Kingdom although all share the same core principles. The Children Acts 1989 and 2004 are the key Acts for England and Wales. The situation is slightly complicated by devolution which has given the National Assembly for Wales the authority to produce the secondary legislation to these statutes so the regulations they pass can differ from those in operation in England. For Scotland, the key legislation is the Children (Scotland) Act 1995 and, for Northern Ireland, it is the Children (Northern Ireland) Order 1995. This section looks at the legislation in England and Wales but a brief synopsis of the law in Scotland is given on p. 172.

The Children Act 1989 is the key piece of legislation for those working with children and families. It seeks to balance the conflicting needs to protect children from family abuse and to protect families from over-intrusion by state agencies. Although the main philosophy is to work in partnership with parents whenever possible, this is not always feasible, and then resort has to be made to legal authority to take the actions thought necessary to ensure a child's safety.

Besides knowing the letter of the law, it is important to understand its spirit and this is captured in the key principles on which it is based:

- The welfare of the child is the paramount consideration. The 'welfare checklist' (Section 1(3)) provides criteria by which judgements about welfare should be made:

  (a) the ascertainable wishes and feelings of the child concerned (considered in the light of his age and understanding);
  (b) his physical, emotional and educational needs;
  (c) the likely effect on him of any change in his circumstances;
  (d) his age, sex, background and any characteristics of his which the court considers relevant;
  (e) any harm which he has suffered or is at risk of suffering;
  (f) how capable each of his parents, and any other person in relation to whom the court considers the question to be relevant, is of meeting his needs;
  (g) the range of powers available to the court under this Act in the proceedings in question.

- Wherever possible, children should be brought up and cared for within their own families.
- Relationship with parents: parents with children in need should be helped to bring up their children themselves; this help would be provided as a service to the child and his family and should:

    – be provided in partnership with the parents;
    – meet each child's identified needs;
    – be appropriate to the child's race, culture, religion and language;
    – be open to effective independent representations and complaints procedures;
    – draw upon effective partnership between the local authority and other agencies, including voluntary agencies.

- Children should be safe and be protected by effective intervention if they are in danger.
- When dealing with children, courts should ensure that delay is avoided (Section 1(2)), and may only make an Order if to do so is better than making no order at all (Section 1(5)).
- Child participation: children should be kept informed about what happens to them, and should participate when decisions are made about their future.

Running theme: the voice of the child

Some children have special needs that must be met if their wishes and feelings are to be ascertained. For some, English is not their first language and so, especially when dealing with a very sensitive personal issue, they may be more able to express themselves in their first language, using interpreters to communicate their views and wishes. Children may also present special needs because they are highly traumatised, whether by the abuse experience itself or other factors in their lives, such as being refugees from a war zone.

Children with disabilities are at higher than average risk of being abused and they may present a variety of challenges to effective communication. A useful resource is a video made by the NSPCC, Triangle and the Joseph Rowntree Foundation called 'Listen to Disabled Children'. The video and accompanying handbook aim to increase professional competence and confidence in communicating with disabled children. For details, see the NSPCC website, www.nspcc. org.uk in the section entitled 'Information resources'.

- Parental responsibility: parents will continue to have parental responsibility for their children, even when their children are no longer living with them. They should be kept informed about their children and participate when decisions are made about their children's future. 'Parental responsibility' is best understood in terms of the range of decisions where it is exercised: determination of the child's religion and education, choosing the child's name, appointing a guardian for the child, consenting to the child's medical treatment and adoption, representing the child in legal proceedings, lawfully correcting the child, protecting and maintaining the child, and having physical possession of the child.

Key sections of the Children Act 1989

Section 17(1) sets out local authorities' duty to help children in need:

> It shall be the general duty of every local authority (in addition to the other duties imposed on them by this part) –
>
> (a)   to safeguard and promote the welfare of children within their area who are in need; and
> (b)   so far as is consistent with that duty, to promote the upbringing of such children by their families, by providing a range and level of services appropriate to those children's needs.

Section 17(10) defines a child in need:

> (a)   he is unlikely to achieve or maintain, or have the opportunity of achieving or maintaining, a reasonable standard of health or development without appropriate provision for him of services by a local authority under this part;
> (b)   his health or development is likely to be significantly impaired, without the provision for him or her of services by a local authority under this Part; or
> (c)   he is disabled.

Section 17(11) includes definitions of terms:

> 'Development' means physical, intellectual, emotional, social or behavioural development; and 'health' means physical or mental health.
>   A disabled child is one who is: blind, deaf or dumb or suffers from mental disorder of any kind, or is substantially and permanently handicapped by illness, injury or congenital or other disability as may be prescribed.

There is no absolute duty to meet the needs of every individual child. The responsibilities of local authorities are set out in qualified terms, for example the local authority shall take *reasonable* steps or shall make provision as they *consider appropriate*. Each local authority sets its own priorities on what needs to meet, linked to the range of services available.

Section 20(1) allows for the accommodation of children by the local authority, on a wholly voluntary basis, as a support service to families in difficulties, akin to the other services that offer support. It should not be looked upon as evidence of parental failure but as evidence of a responsible attitude to the discharge of parental duties. Section 20(1) reads:

Every local authority shall provide accommodation for any child in need within their area who appears to them to require accommodation as a result of (a) there being no person who has parental responsibility for him; (b) his being lost or having been abandoned; or (c) the person who has been caring for him being prevented (whether or not permanently, and for whatever reason) from providing him with suitable accommodation or care.

Section 47 sets out the duties and powers in relation to protecting children from abuse and neglect.

(1) Where a local authority –

    (a) are informed that a child who lives, or is found, in their area -

        (i) is the subject of an emergency protection order; or
        (ii) is in police protection; or

    (b) have reasonable cause to suspect that a child who lives, or is found, in their area is suffering, or is likely to suffer, significant harm,

the authority shall make, or cause to be made, such inquiries as they consider necessary to enable them to decide whether they should take any action to safeguard or promote the child's welfare.

Central to the local authority's inquiries is the need to see the child, unless they are satisfied that they have sufficient information already (Section 47(4)).

Compulsory intervention on child protection grounds

Although the central philosophy of the legislation is to work in partnership with parents, there are a number of legal orders that can be used if this approach fails to allow a S47 inquiry to be conducted or fails to ensure the safety of the child. The key orders are listed below.

Emergency Protection Powers

Emergency Protection Orders (EPO):

The court may make an emergency protection order under section 44 of the Children Act 1989 if it is satisfied that there is reasonable cause to believe that a child is likely to suffer significant harm if:

- he is not removed to accommodation; or
- he does not remain in the place in which he is then being accommodated.

An emergency protection order may also be made if S47 inquiries are being frustrated by access to the child being unreasonably refused to a person authorised to seek access, and the applicant has reasonable cause to believe that access is needed as a matter of urgency.

An emergency protection order gives authority to remove a child, and places the child under the protection of the applicant for a maximum of eight days (with a possible extension of up to seven days).

Exclusion Requirement

The court may include an exclusion requirement in an emergency protection order or an interim care order (S38(a) and 44(a) of the Children Act 1989). This allows a perpetrator to be removed from the home instead of having to remove the child. The court must be satisfied that:

- there is reasonable cause to believe that if the person is excluded from the home in which the child lives, the child will cease to suffer, or cease to be likely to suffer, significant harm or that enquiries will cease to be frustrated; and
- another person living in the home is able and willing to give the child the care which it would be reasonable to expect a parent to give, and consents to the exclusion requirement.

Police Protection Powers

Under S46 of the Children Act 1989, where a police officer has reasonable cause to believe that a child would otherwise be likely to suffer significant harm, he or she may:

- remove the child to suitable accommodation and keep him or her there; or
- take reasonable steps to ensure that the child's removal from any hospital, or other place in which the child is then being accommodated, is prevented.

No child may be kept in police protection for more than 72 hours.

Non-emergency powers

S43(1) The Child Assessment Order (CAO)

This covers cases where there has been a repeated failure to produce a child so professionals cannot be assured of the child's safety and welfare *but* the matter is not so urgent as to require an EPO. It allows for an assessment of the child to take place.

S31(2) Care Orders

These orders allow for the extreme measure of coercively removing a child from parental care. The grounds for them are:

> (a) that the child concerned is suffering, or is likely to suffer, significant harm; and (b) that the harm, or likelihood of harm, is attributable to (i) the care given to the child, or likely to be given to him if the order were not made, not being what it would be reasonable to expect a parent to give to him; or (ii) the child's being beyond parental control.

Care plans: Under an amendment to the Children Act 1989 in the Adoption and Children Act 2002, care plans are now required. The local authority has to submit a care plan to the court, setting out how it intends to handle the upbringing of the child in the event of a care order being made.

The legal impact of a care order is set out in Section 33: the local authority 'shall have parental responsibility for the child', that is, 'all the rights, duties, powers, responsibilities and authority which by law a parent of a child has in relation to the child and his property'. There are some specific exemptions, for example the local authority cannot change the religion, does not acquire the rights to have the child adopted, cannot appoint a guardian for the child, or change their surname.

Future contact between the child and parents should be considered before a care order is made: Section 34(1) states:

> Before making a care order with respect to any child the court shall – (a) consider the arrangements which the authority have made, or propose to make, for affording any person contact with a child to whom this section applies; and (b) invite the parties to the proceedings to comment on those arrangements.

Duration of a care order: unless it is brought to an end earlier, a care order will continue in force until the child reaches the age of 18 (S19(12)).

S38 Interim Care Orders (ICO)

The court can make an interim care order in two situations:

1. Where an application has been made for a care order or supervision order and that application is adjourned by the court.

2. Where there are family proceedings (e.g. divorce) before a court and the court decides under Section 37 to order the local authority to investigate the possibility of applying for compulsory powers.

As their name implies, interim care orders are only short-term measures, and will last for as long as the court says, but this cannot be more than a maximum of eight weeks, or until a full order is made. Subsequent interim care orders can be applied for, for a maximum of four weeks each.

S31 Supervision Orders

These have the same threshold criteria as care orders in terms of significant harm but confer the duty on the supervisor to 'advise assist and befriend' the supervised child.

Schedule 3 specifies various types of requirements that may be included in a supervision order, the key feature being flexibility. For example:

- the child is to live at a place or places as directed by the supervisor for a specified period;
- the child is to present himself to a person as directed by the supervisor at specified places on specified days;
- the child is to participate in activities as directed by the supervisor on specified days;
- the 'responsible person' – this is any person having parental responsibility – is to take all reasonable steps to ensure the child complies with any direction given by the supervisor for the purpose of taking part in specified activities, or for medical examinations. He/she should also keep the supervisor informed of any change of address.

Duration: Schedule 3, paragraph 6 stipulates that a supervision order shall cease to have effect at the end of one year beginning with the date on which it was made. The supervisor can apply for one or more extensions up to a three-year period.

Sanctions: the legal position on sanctions was spelled out by the Court of Appeal in the case of R v.*[1996] 2 FCR 555:* if a parent or child fails to comply with the requirements of a supervision order, then the supervisor may return to court. There the ultimate sanction will be the making of a care order under which the local authority will be given the necessary legal powers to enforce its will.

The principle of inter-professional collaboration is given statutory footing in Section 47(9), which provides for the following to assist with the local authority's inquiries, unless to do so would be unreasonable in all the circumstances of the case: any local authority, any local education authority, any local housing authority, any health authority, and any other person authorised by the Secretary of State.

Working Together to Safeguard Children 2006b. The first edition of this guidance was published in 1991, with major amendments in 1999 to take account of the changes introduced by the Children Act 1989. The latest edition (2006b) reflects the changes in the Children Act 2004 and the safeguarding agenda. There is an increased emphasis on inter-agency co-operation for dealing with all concerns about a child's health and development, and responding to concerns about significant harm from child abuse and neglect is located within this wider framework.

Children Act 2004

For the most part, this covers different aspects of the law from the Children Act 1989 and so is more of an addition than an amendment to that statute. Part 1 makes provision for the establishment of a Children's Commissioner for England (commissioners already exist in the other three countries). Part 2 strengthens the duty for agencies to work together to promote children's welfare. It replaces Area Child Protection Committees with Local Safeguarding Children's Boards, statutory bodies with greater power and responsibility. It authorises the appointment of 'Children's Directors' in local authorities, merging education and social care. Section 12 authorises the setting-up of a national index containing basic data on all children; agencies will be required to register their involvement with a child on the index and can enter an 'indication' if they want others to know that they have made an assessment, are taking action, or have information to share. The regulations for this index will be published in 2006.

 Taking it **FURTHER**

Some commentators have argued that there is a fundamental division between legal and child welfare discourses in the way that they conceptualise children. The legal discourse is concerned with determining what is the correct legal decision, and this can be at odds with social workers' judgements about the welfare needs of the child. As a result legal decision making may not always reflect what social workers consider to be the best interests of the child and this can be a cause of frustration and discomfort (Wall, 2000). Why might a therapeutic goal for a child conflict with the legally 'correct' one? Do social workers have different standards of evidence, or different overall goals from lawyers and judges? See M. King and C. Piper (1995) *How the Law Thinks about Children*, Aldershot: Ashgate, for a full discussion.

Further Reading

A. BRAMMER (2003) *Social Work Law, Harlow: Pearson Education Ltd. A comprehensive guide to the law and the workings of the legal system, with Part 2 dealing specifically with children and families. It defines legal terms well and provides clear accounts of the principles underlying legislation.*

N. ALLEN (2005) *Making Sense of the Children Act 1989, 4th edn, Chichester: Wiley. This is a very accessible text, explaining the law and making links to practice issues.*

N. WALL (2000) *A Handbook for Expert Witnesses in Children Act Cases, Bristol: Jordan. A useful guide for those who have to appear in court.*

Full texts of individual laws can be obtained from www.opsi.gov.uk/acts.

2.4	
dealing with uncertainty	

Learning outcomes

This section will help you to understand:

- The unavoidable element of uncertainty in child protection work.

- The importance of the organisational culture and support in helping front-line workers deal with uncertainty.

- The place of tools and procedures within good practice.

- The importance of keeping good records.

- The common errors of reasoning in making judgements and decisions.

Human beings yearn for the security of certainty but this can be dangerous in child protection work. Practitioners have to make judgements and decisions on the basis of limited knowledge and need to remain aware of the possibility that they have made a mistake. Being able to tolerate a degree of uncertainty is a core requirement in good practice, to maintain what Lord Laming called 'respectful uncertainty' and 'healthy scepticism' (Laming, 2003). The alternative is to form a picture of a family and then close your mind to any alternative account; any evidence that challenges your opinion is rejected or devalued instead of being given serious consideration.

Cooper, Hetherington and Katz (2003: 47) sum up the problem for child welfare practitioners:

> At the core of the problem of child welfare systems is the need for practitioners, and therefore the system, to be open to working in both a supportive and suspicious frame of mind at the same time. ... Supportive relationships are based on trust; suspicious relationships are based on mistrust. Trust can occur within the context of a suspicious relationship but it is conditional and tentative. Managing these tensions is central to the professional skill of the social worker.

In practice, it is very hard for practitioners to move between the mind-sets of support and suspicion. As reviews of child abuse inquiries have found, once an opinion of a family is formed, practitioners find it hard to revise it, whatever new information comes up (Munro, 1999).

In the case of Stephanie Fox, who had been removed from her parents because of abuse, practitioners judged that her parents were subsequently working well with them and making progress. Stephanie was returned to their care. She then suffered a series of injuries, all explained as accidental. Each was taken in isolation and the parents' explanation accepted. Nursery staff tried to raise concern about her but their efforts were dismissed and the optimistic opinion of the parents prevailed. In total, thirty reports of bruises and burns were made before Stephanie was killed by a head injury. (Wandsworth Area Child Protection Committee, 1989)

In the current policy of early intervention and working supportively with families, managing this duality of support and suspicion becomes a duty for all practitioners working with families. Although working primarily in partnership, they have to be aware that abuse or neglect are possible explanations of the perceived problems and refer to social care agencies if there is a concern about significant harm.

Decisions have to be made at every stage with less than perfect knowledge. We have limited knowledge of:

- what is happening in the child's life
- what will happen if we do nothing
- what will happen if we take a particular course of action.

Consequently, the judgements and decisions that are essential in making plans to protect a child all contain a degree of uncertainty. Given this, the public's harsh reaction when mistakes are made and a child dies can seem unreasonable. They, however, have the benefit of hindsight and hindsight can make everyone wise. Looking back, it is easy to see the real significance of information, to know what was trivial and what was important, to understand the true meaning of ambiguous bits of evidence, and to see what the professionals *should have done* if they had had your accurate understanding of the case. With only the benefits of foresight, the world is much more confusing and puzzling. This chapter details the factors that are considered helpful in reducing uncertainty and that contribute to decisions being made in a way that is clear and accountable.

Tools, skills and human rationality

Tools are becoming a major factor in practice in children's services. A range of tools – assessment frameworks, recording formats, computer databases – have been developed to help front-line workers and their managers. The Integrated Children's System (ICS), for example, contains sets of forms covering the main stages in social work involvement in a range of types of cases. To understand how such tools can support practice, it is useful to look at human rationality and identify how tools interact with human skills and knowledge.

There have been two main approaches to studying how people reason: the analytic and the intuitive. Analytic reasoning is formal, explicit and logical. It is associated with mathematics and rigorous thought, where every step in the argument is spelled out. Intuitive reasoning, in contrast, is inarticulate, swiftly reaching a conclusion on the basis of largely unconscious processes, for example forming an opinion of a person as we talk to them.

Both approaches to reasoning are clearly visible in social work and child protection. The advocates of a more analytic approach stress the benefits of checklists, frameworks and procedures for making the process of work visible and systematic and for also encouraging consistent practice. Those who value intuitive reasoning stress its importance in understanding our fellow human beings, of appreciating how they feel, how their culture influences their behaviour, and why they took the course of action they did. Although the reasoning styles are sometimes presented as stark opposites so that people are asked to take sides, it is more accurate to see them as on a continuum, not as a dichotomy

(Hammond, 1996). This way of looking at reasoning skills allows for more subtle questions to be asked about the merits of each type of reasoning at different stages of the child protection process and opens up the possibility of shifting reasoning in one direction or the other.

By making reasoning in child protection work as explicit and open as possible, judgements and decisions can be tested, challenged and understood by others, not least by the families involved. While such rigorous thinking cannot remove uncertainty, it can reduce it and it can also make judgements and decisions understandable and defensible – the only true defence available to a professional in the tragic event of a child's death.

However, this does not mean that more intuitive reasoning should be excluded or belittled. It is, in particular, essential in developing relationship skills, in talking to children and parents, and gaining their co-operation sufficiently to be able to give and collect information. Without a high level of interviewing skill, professionals will have a limited ability to get the basic data necessary to record in the various documents or to engage the family in a constructive working relationship to tackle problems.

Moreover, intuitive thinking is not irrational or mysterious. On reflection, it is possible for the thinker to unpack the judgement to identify the evidence that led to it. One of the functions of supervision is to help the worker reflect in this way so that their reasoning is more open to critical review (Fook, 2002).

The tools that are being adopted in children's services will only help to improve practice if they are used purposefully by skilled professionals. The tools provide valuable checklists of what areas of information might be useful and they encourage systematic thinking about a family. They do not, however, do the hard work. The professionals have to find the information, they have to interpret its significance, and they have to make the difficult judgements and decisions that determine how the case progresses (Munro, 2002).

Organisational culture

The professional working with a family is not an isolated individual but the visible representative of the whole system. It has increasingly become recognised that how individuals behave, the quality of their work, is powerfully influenced by how the system supports them.

> The more that workers are cared for, nurtured and protected, the more they will be able to provide this for the children they serve. (Ferguson, 2005: 794)

The professional who has had appropriate training, has access to the necessary resources, and who is given clear and achievable goals by the senior management is going to offer a better service to the family than the professional who is struggling with tasks beyond his or her skill, who has no supervision or services to draw on, and who feels confused by conflicting, over-ambitious goals.

Blame: many working in social care experience a blame culture, in which people become defensive and hide any hesitations they may have or cover up any slips they might have made. This operates against good, critical thinking since its hallmark is openness to error and a willingness to re-think one's judgements and decisions.

A learning organisation: this tries to create the opposite environment for the workforce, in which the complexity and fallibility of the work is recognised and individuals are encouraged to give honest feedback to their managers about their experiences at the front line.

Emotional intelligence: to tolerate the discomfort of uncertainty and remain open to new evidence or new ideas, emotional intelligence is needed but this needs to be at the organisational as well as the individual level. Front-line workers can only realistically practise at such a high level of skill if they are operating in an organisation that has the culture and the resources to support them.

Supervision: one lesson repeated in numerous child abuse inquiries is the crucial role of supervision in offering a setting in which the front-line worker can be helped to look more objectively and critically at their reasoning processes. An organisation which allows supervision to become focused on managerial issues without time and attention given to the casework process deprives the front-line staff of a crucial resource.

Running theme: emotional impact

Individuals should not be expected to cope on their own. The employing agency has a responsibility to provide the support and supervision needed to manage the intellectual and emotional demands of the job. Burnout in workers is the extreme product of a failure to provide an adequately supportive environment. Maslach et al. (2001) define burnout as having three dimensions: emotional exhaustion, depersonalisation (or cynicism) and reduced personal accomplishment. Exhaustion is the main feature, prompting people to distance themselves emotionally from the work, and from the children and parents they are supposed to help. The factors that lead to burnout lie more in the organisational context than in the personality of the workers:

- feeling there is too much work to do in the time available;
- experiencing the conflict of having to meet competing demands;
- role ambiguity is also a source of stress – not being given enough information to do the job properly;
- a lack of social support, especially support from supervisors, contributes to burnout. People's degree of control over their work also matters – getting feedback on what has been done, being involved in decision making, and feeling autonomous all have a positive impact on morale;
- working intensively with people in a caregiving role is emotionally challenging and leads to higher rates of burnout.

Individual characteristics of the worker, such as being young and being unmarried, have some significance but are not as important as situational factors in producing burnout.

Recording

The human short-term memory can handle seven items of information (give or take two) so it is crucial to keep a record of key information and to refer to it when discussing a case. Current impressions of a family need to be systematically checked against what was written in the past because, in our memory, the present tends to obscure or colour the past.

Key resource: www.writeenough.org.uk is an excellent website providing an interactive training pack, commissioned by the Children's Services Division of the DfES. It provides guidance on what to record, how to differentiate fact and opinion, and how and when to respect confidentiality. Common pitfalls in recording are listed:

- The child is 'missing' from the record.
- Case records are out of date.
- Facts and professional judgements are not distinguished in the record.
- The size of the record makes it difficult to manage.
- There is no assessment on file.
- The record is not written for sharing.
- The record is not used as a tool for analysis.
- The record is disrespectful to the service user.

Another common pitfall cited in several studies is that records tend to be biased towards recording the dramatic information, and, without adequate description of the less vivid details and the contextual details, these can be easily misinterpreted by others reading the record (Herrenkohl, 2005: 420).

Common errors of reasoning

Human beings are not passive observers of the world but active seekers of meaning and of patterns. Early textbooks in social work advised workers to look first and theorise later. This is humanly impossible. We think, conjecture, make sense of whatever we experience as automatically as we breathe. Try to meet a family and just observe without making any judgements.

This active approach to experience is not, in itself, a problem but we need to be cautious and remember how fallible these instant opinions are. Many of the mistakes that are made in practice are not random but predictable because they arise from the shortcuts that people tend to take in reasoning. The world is full of information and noise; shortcuts are used to cut the thinking task down to a human size that is manageable in the time available. Some shortcuts are very common in human reasoning and, most of the time, they are very useful and efficient, helping us to reach judgements and decisions quickly. However, they also produce predictable biases in the way we think and, in child protection work, we need to be aware of these biases and try to counteract them.

Resistance to changing our minds

This is a pervasive and problematic aspect of human reasoning. People, once they have formed a point of view about a family, are remarkably resistant to revising their opinion even when presented with what seems like overwhelming evidence against it. The mistake shows up repeatedly in inquiries into child abuse deaths (Munro, 1999).

There are a number of strategies for blocking out information that does not fit with the current point of view:

- avoidance – for example not talking to the school to check the mother's story;
- forgetting – so the information does not influence your thinking;
- rejecting – finding some reason for invalidating the information, for example that the neighbour who told you is malicious;
- re-interpreting – giving the information a new meaning that is benign instead of worrying.

How to counteract: strenuous efforts have been made to find ways of dealing with this bias and two strategies seem most effective:

1 Bringing in a fresh pair of eyes to consider the case. This can be a feature of supervision and of review meetings and recognises how hard it is for the person involved with a family to stand back and look at them objectively.

2 Playing devil's advocate: deliberately trying to defend the opposite point of view. This seems to work by helping you see information that tells against your opinion or suggesting alternative interpretations of the evidence.

Running theme: the voice of the child

Because of their low status, children are particularly vulnerable to having their evidence dismissed if it does not support the professionals' existing opinion. Analysis of the occasions in child abuse inquiries, where children's version of events had been sought, found that practitioners tended to believe them if what they said agreed with their own views and disbelieve them when their account conflicted (Munro, 1999).

Selective use of information

Some kinds of information come more readily to mind so that they have undue weight in people's reasoning. People find it easiest to recall details that are:

- vivid, not dull;
- concrete, not abstract;
- emotion-laden, not neutral;
- recent, not distant; except that ...
- first impressions have an enduring impact.

How to counteract

In assessing and reviewing cases, it is essential not to rely on memory or this bias will operate at full strength. Good records, that include the details that are easily forgotten, and checklists, that remind the professional of the range of factors to take into account, provide good counterbalances.

 Taking it **FURTHER**

One destructive way of dealing with uncertainty in child protection practice is to develop defensive practice which typically takes two forms: (i) erring always on the side of caution so that children are removed from their parents at a low threshold of risk (after a major child abuse tragedy, you will often see a rise in the numbers of children removed); and (ii) sticking rigidly and mechanistically to procedures and protocols with the mistaken view that, as long as all the forms are completed within the timetable, the professional will be safe from criticism. What are the defects with these two strategies? What harm might arise from removing children at a low threshold? If procedures represent 'best practice', is it ever justified to not comply with them?

Further Reading

J. FOOK **(2002)** *Social Work: critical theory and practice, London: Sage Publications. Offers a detailed account of critical reflective practice.*

G. MACDONALD **(2001)** *Effective Interventions for Child Abuse and Neglect, Chichester: Wiley. Chapter 12 provides a good discussion of the nature of assessment and the research findings on what makes for a good or inadequate assessment.*

E. MUNRO **(2002)** *Effective Child Protection, London: Sage Publications. Covers the skills needed in assessing risk and making decisions. Chapter 8 is on common errors and how to minimise them.*

2.5

using research

Learning outcomes

This section will help you understand:

- The importance of evaluating work with families.

- How using research can strengthen your practice.

- How to find research studies to help you with a particular case.

- How to read research and judge how reliable the findings are.

Reviews of child abuse services conclude that most services being offered to families are not based on any clear evidence that the services actually work (Chaffin and Friedrich, 2004). In most cases, this is due to a lack of research rather than any evidence that the services are ineffective. There is, however, some relevant research available which professionals should know and use. Moreover, research is a rapidly growing resource, driven not only by professionals wishing to learn about what works but also by politicians wanting to check if public money is being spent effectively.

Since the users of child protection services are among the most vulnerable and powerless in society, there are strong moral as well as technical arguments for checking the impact of professional interventions and for using the interventions with most demonstrated evidence of success.

Good intentions do not guarantee good outcomes

It cannot, in addition, be assumed that interventions are, at the worst, ineffective. Studies have found harmful effects as well as beneficial ones.

> An early attempt at preventing delinquency in the USA provides a salutary example. In the 1930s, 300 boys in a particular area were identified as 'at risk' of becoming delinquent. They were randomly allocated to two groups, one of which received individual help and, where needed, referral to specialist services. The control group received no additional help. Many in the experimental group thought the preventive service had been helpful. When followed up in the 1970s, it was found that those who had received help were *more likely* to have been convicted of a crime, to have died, on average, five years earlier, and were more likely to have been diagnosed as alcoholic, schizophrenic, or manic-depressive. (McCord, 1992)

The role of research has been emphasised in recent policy statements and it is now a clear requirement in training for social work and for all professional groups working with children (DfES, 2005). However, research does not produce simple recipes for action. Professionals need to read it critically and decide how it is relevant to the families with whom they are working. The research process should not look unfamiliar to practitioners because, in many ways, it echoes the social work process. Tripodi (1974) highlighted the similarities:

Social Work:		*Research:*
Assessment	⟺	*Problem formulation*
Determine intervention plan	⟺	*Research strategy*
Implement intervention	⟺	*Collect data*
Evaluate intervention effects	⟺	*Analysis of data*
Review and termination	⟺	*Conclusions*

This section examines the two major approaches to using research in practice: evidence-based practice and evidence-informed practice.

Evidence-based practice

This approach was developed in medicine and has been adapted to the social care context. It brings together three key components in decision making:

1 the best available research evidence;

2 the practitioner's professional judgement of the particular case;

3 the service user's values and preferences.

Drawing on all these elements, the practitioner makes a decision about how to help the service user. At its best, evidence-based practice empowers service users by tailoring help to their values and wishes, and offers them the help that, on balance, looks most likely to be successful. At its worst, evidence-based practice is used mechanistically, looking only at the research evidence, deciding what works best for a class of problems, and applying it to the particular case, whatever the views or the unique characteristics of the service user.

The main stages of an evidence-based approach are:

- converting a need for information into an answerable question;
- finding the relevant research evidence;
- critically appraising that evidence to judge how reliable it is;
- judging whether it can be applied to the particular service user;

- judging whether it is appropriate, in the light of the service user's values and preferences;
- taking action based on this appraisal;
- evaluating the outcome.

The first three stages – of finding and critiquing the best available research evidence – are the aspects that mark this approach out from traditional practice and require new skills.

Converting a need for information into an answerable question

The five most common types of question front-line workers are likely to have are:

1 *Effectiveness questions*: how effective would this particular inter-vention be for this particular service user, e.g. how well will par-enting classes address the specific problems of this service user?

2 *Risk/prognosis questions*: how likely is it that a particular person will engage in a particular behaviour, e.g. re-abuse their child?

3 *Description questions*: how common is this problem, e.g. how many teenagers take soft drugs?

4 *Assessment questions*: how can I most accurately describe the service user's problems, e.g. is there a reliable measure of depression?

5 *Prevention questions*: how can I most effectively prevent this problem from occurring, e.g. what strategies will most effectively prevent teenagers dropping out of school?

(Adapted from Gibbs and Gambrill, 1999)

Finding the relevant research evidence

The Internet has transformed practitioners' access to research. It not only allows access to a vast range of data but is continually updated and so contains the latest results. A number of websites have been developed with the specific goal of meeting practitioners' need for convenient access to the findings of research. They provide guidance on how to use the resources as well as links to relevant research webpages. Many include summaries of research findings, drawing out their implications for practice.

www.scie-socialcareonline.org.uk An excellent website with a wealth of material. In the 'Training and learning' section, there are links to online tutorials to help you improve your Internet skills, learn how to formulate key words so that you make the best use of search engines to locate relevant research, and appraise critically research studies once found.

www.scie.org.uk The website of the Social Care Institute for Excellence. Besides operating social care online (see above), SCIE aims to improve the experience of people who use social care by developing and promoting knowledge about good practice in the sector. They publish four series: Research Briefings, Reports, Practice Guides and Resource Guides.

www.whatworksforchildren.org.uk This is an ESRC-funded website that contains an Evidence Guide, offering advice on how to find and critique research. It also has a useful set of 'Evidence Nuggets' – summaries of research evidence on some specific interventions, for example cognitive behavioural therapies and home visiting.

www.campbellcollaboration.org This is an international non-profit organisation that aims to help people make well-informed decisions about the effects of interventions in the social, behavioural and educational arenas. It contains a Register of Randomised Controlled Trials and prepares systematic reviews of studies of interventions. In the Social Welfare section, there are a number of reviews of relevance to child welfare. Many more are in the process of being conducted so this site will become increasingly useful.

http://nccanch.acf.hhs.gov The website for the National Clearinghouse on Child Abuse and Neglect, an American organisation. Besides a wide range of material on identifying and responding to child abuse and neglect, it has in the 'For Professionals' section a category called 'Promising Practices' – a list of publications and other web resources on promising and emerging practices in child protection.

www.cwla.org The Child Welfare League of America's website has an extensive set of relevant material and a section called 'Research to practice initiative' that contains a number of reports summarising research on specific issues and discussing their relevance to practice.

www.rom.ku.edu/EBP_main.asp An American website containing an evidence-based practice tool, offering summaries of research evidence on six major practice issues: timely reunification, maintaining permanency upon leaving care, timely adoption, placement stability, preventing maltreatment recurrence, and child safety in care. Although written in the language of the American child welfare system, it is easy to see where and how it is relevant to the UK system.

Critically appraising the evidence

All research has some defects if examined closely enough. The demands and complexities of the real world make some compromises in methodology unavoidable. However, this does not mean that all studies are equally bad. Users of evidence need to be able to look at how the study was conducted and judge how reliable its findings are. There cannot be a simple hierarchy of research methods because the type of method used is influenced by the type of question asked. A study aimed at finding out how parents experience home visiting will have a different design from one that aims to find out whether home visiting reduces abuse. The different research designs suit different research questions.

Detailed information on critiquing research can be obtained from the Public Health Resources Unit, which has a Learning and Development section that includes a set of appraisal tools for each of the main research designs. Available at: www.phru.nhs.uk/casp.

Also relevant is Chapter 3, 'Critical appraisal: sorting the wheat from the chaff', in Newman et al., 2005.

Gambrill (2003) summarises the arguments for evidence-based social work:

- helping clients develop critical appraisal skills
- involving clients in design and critique of practice and policy related research
- involving clients as informed participants who share in decision making
- recognising client's unique knowledge in terms of application concerns
- promoting transparency and honesty
- encouraging a systemic approach for integrating practical, ethical and evidentiary issues
- maximising the flow of knowledge and information about knowledge gaps.

Challenges in developing evidence-based practice:

1 Organisational culture: front-line workers need the support of their organisation to practise in an evidence-based way. The organisation not only needs to provide practical resources, such as good Internet access and supervisory support, but also needs to have a culture that values evidence-based practice so that finding time for it is a high priority, not a luxury to be fitted in after meeting other commitments. A practice guide to organisational support for using research evidence has been produced by Research in Practice (2006).

2 Workforce skills: evidence-based practice needs practitioners who have the skills and motivation to seek out, critique, and use evidence to help their service users.

3 Limitations of child protection research: in its current state, the body of research available is limited, partly by difficulties inherent in the subject matter and partly by the limited progress that has been made in developing a knowledge base. Macdonald (2001: 19) lists the problems:

- A paucity of studies of adequate methodological rigour and sample size.
- Variations in the definitions of abuse and neglect used in different studies making comparison difficult.
- Variations in the assumed causation of abuse so that different aspects of families are examined in different studies.
- Variations in the range, relevance and reliability of the outcome measures used.
- A failure to say precisely what the intervention is that is being evaluated so that it is difficult for others to copy it.
- A tendency to use a mix of methods so that the contribution of any one to the overall outcome is unclear.
- The populations studied are rarely large and the samples are rarely selected randomly, leading to skewed samples that limit the generalisability of the results.
- A range of methodological weaknesses in the studies, such as a high drop-out rate.
- A preponderance of studies where the families have less serious problems than those typically encountered in the child protection system, with services often being offered in more controlled environments than normal working conditions.

Evidence-informed practice

Where the evidence-based practice approach sees the social worker making an independent assessment of the evidence and tailoring it to the specific values and wishes of the service user, the evidence-informed approach has a more modest ambition of encouraging professionals to use theories and interventions that have been judged by others to be well-evidenced.

Arguments for

Evidence-informed practice is all that can realistically be expected of social workers, few of whom have the time, motivation, resources or skills to seek out and critique research for themselves.

The growing trend in producing digests of research findings makes it even easier for workers and agencies to adopt this approach (see websites listed above).

It has the same benefit as evidence-based practice in using research findings on effectiveness in deciding how to help service users.

Arguments against

It runs the danger of pushing the service user's wishes out of the equation as it encourages acceptance of an intervention for a category of people and is not sensitive to the unique aspects of the individual.

It just replaces one authority (tradition) with another (the judgement of researchers) instead of making practitioners themselves authoritative users of research.

There is clearly a continuum between the two approaches and it is perhaps most realistic to expect that professionals will begin with evidence-informed practice and gradually become more authoritative users of research as they become more familiar with research and more confident in judging its relevance for themselves. Their organisations will play a central part in encouraging or discouraging critical and thorough use of research.

 Taking it **FURTHER**

There has long been a debate in social work about whether it is possible to carry out empirical research on the subtle nuances of practice. It has been argued that it is a mistake to model social work knowledge on the natural sciences because the subject matter – of human happiness and welfare – is intrinsically different. Intuition and empathy are seen as the key skills for understanding our fellow human beings, not empirical scientific methods. Do you think that research is too blunt an instrument to capture social work practice? Alternatively, is it irresponsible *not* to study the impact professionals have on families? For a full discussion, see E. Munro (1998) *Understanding Social Work: an empirical approach*, London: Continuum Press.

Further Reading

P. MARSH AND M. FISHER (2005) *Developing the Evidence Base for Social Work and Social Care Practice, SCIE Using Knowledge in Social Care Report 10,* London: SCIE.

T. NEWMAN, A. MOSELEY, S. TIERNEY AND A. ELLIS **(2005)** *Evidence-based Social Work: a guide for the perplexed, Lyme Regis: Russell House Publishing. A very practical manual to help social workers gain their confidence in finding and using research.*

D. SACKETT, S. STRAUSS, W. RICHARDSON, W. ROSENBERG AND R. HAYNES **(2000)** *Evidence-based Medicine: how to practise and teach EBM, London: Churchill Livingstone. This is a seminal work in medicine, setting out the key principles of evidence-based medicine.*

2.6	
what is child abuse and neglect?	

Learning outcomes

This section will help you to understand:

- The concept of child abuse is socially constructed and varies over time, within societies, and between societies.

- The right to protection from abuse is established in the UN Convention on the Rights of the Child.

- The application of the general definitions of abuse and neglect to particular cases can be very problematic.

- The importance of understanding the culture of the family in making judgements about the meaning of their behaviour.

- When given statistics on the incidence of abuse, you need to ask what definition was used and how the data was gathered.

Defining abuse

At its simplest, child abuse can be defined as ways of treating children that are harmful and morally wrong. However, ideas of what is harmful and wrong vary over time, between cultures and between people. Even within one cultural group, there is considerable disagreement on the fine detail of how children should be cared for. For example how much discipline is desirable and when does it tip over into being too much? What is the balance of risk and benefit from babies sleeping with their parents?

Concern about child abuse seems to have followed a common path of development in societies, from a concern first about serious physical abuse and neglect, then widened to include emotional abuse and then sexual abuse. The definitions of abuse have also tended to expand to include lower levels of maltreatment.

The widest definition of abuse that I have come across is that used by the British National Commission of Inquiry into the Prevention of Child Abuse:

> Child abuse consists of anything which individuals, institutions, or processes do or fail to do which directly or indirectly harms children or damages their prospects of safe and healthy development into adulthood. (National Commission, 1996: 2)

In this broad sense, 'protecting children from abuse' is equivalent to current policy's phrase 'safeguarding from harm'. They both refer to *all* factors that have an adverse impact on children's health and development. However, such a broad definition of abuse is unusual and potentially confusing so, within this book, it is not used. Child protection refers to the subsections within 'safeguarding from harm' where the actions and inactions of individuals are implicated. *How* individuals are implicated is one of the issues that will be explored in this chapter.

International definitions; United Nations Convention on the Rights of the Child

Child abuse has received worldwide condemnation, and protection from abuse is included in the United Nations Convention on the Rights of the Child. This is the most widely supported UN convention, having been ratified by every country except the United States of America and Somalia who have both indicated their intention to ratify by taking the initial step of signing the convention.

The World Health Organisation (www.who.int) has produced definitions of abuse and neglect that aim to be applicable to all countries, whatever their culture or level of economic development:

General definition: child abuse or maltreatment consists of 'all forms of physical and/or emotional ill-treatment, sexual abuse, neglect or negligent treatment or commercial or other exploitation resulting in actual or potential harm to the child's health, survival, development or dignity in the context of a relationship of responsibility, trust, or power'.

Clarifications:

Physical abuse of a child is that which results in actual or potential physical harm from an interaction or lack of interaction, which is reasonably within the control of a parent or person in a position of responsibility, power or trust. There may be single or repeated incidents.

Emotional abuse includes the failure to provide a developmentally appropriate, supportive environment, including the availability of a primary attachment figure, so that the child can develop a stable and full range of emotional and social competencies commensurate with her or his personal potential, and in the context of the society in which the child dwells. There may also be acts toward the child that cause or have a high probability of causing harm to the child's health or physical, mental, spiritual, moral or social development. These acts must be reasonably within the control of the parent or person in a relationship of responsibility, trust or power. Acts include restriction of movement, patterns of belittling, denigrating, scape-goating, threatening, scaring, discriminating, ridiculing or other non-physical forms of hostile or rejecting treatment.

Neglect and negligent treatment is the inattention or omission on the part of the caregiver to provide for the development of the child in all spheres: health, education, emotional development, nutrition, shelter, and safe living conditions, in the context of the resources reasonably available to the family or caretakers and causes, or has a high probability of causing, harm to the child's health or physical, mental, spiritual, moral or social development. This includes the failure to properly supervise and protect children from harm as much as is feasible.

Sexual abuse is the involvement of a child in sexual activity that he or she does not fully comprehend, is unable to give informed consent to, or for which the child is not developmentally prepared and cannot give consent, or that violate the laws or social taboos of society. Child sexual abuse is evidenced by an activity between a child and an adult or another child who by age or development is in a relationship of responsibility, trust or power, the activity being intended to gratify or satisfy the needs of the other person. This may include but is not limited to the inducement or coercion of a child to engage in any unlawful sexual activity; the exploitative use of child in prostitution or other unlawful sexual practices; the exploitative use of children in pornographic performances and materials.

Exploitation: commercial or other exploitation of a child refers to use of the child in work or other activities for the benefit of others. This includes, but is not limited to, child labour and child prostitution. These activities are to the detriment of the child's physical or mental health, education, moral or social-emotional development.

In the UK, the official definitions of abuse and neglect contained in *Working Together to Safeguard Children* (DfES, 2006: 8) are similar but slightly less detailed:

What is Abuse and Neglect?

1.27   Abuse and neglect are forms of maltreatment of a child. Somebody may abuse or neglect a child by inflicting harm, or by failing to act to prevent harm. Children may be abused in a family or an institutional or community setting; by those known to them or, more rarely, by a stranger. They may be abused by an adult or adults or another child or children.

Physical Abuse

1.28   Physical abuse may involve hitting, shaking, throwing, poisoning, burning or scalding, drowning, suffocating, or otherwise causing physical harm to a child. Physical harm may also be caused when a parent or carer fabricates the symptoms of, or deliberately induces illness in, a child.

Emotional Abuse

1.29   Emotional abuse is the persistent emotional maltreatment of a child such as to cause severe and persistent adverse effects on the child's emotional development. It may involve conveying to children that they are worthless or unloved, inadequate, or valued only insofar as they meet the needs of another person. It may feature age or developmentally inappropriate expectations being imposed on children. These may include interactions that are beyond the child's developmental capability, as well as overprotection and limitation of exploration and learning, or preventing the child participating in normal social interaction. It may involve seeing or hearing the ill-treatment of another. It may involve causing children frequently to feel frightened or in danger, or the exploitation or corruption of children. Some level of emotional abuse is involved in all types of maltreatment of a child, though it may occur alone.

Sexual Abuse

1.30   Sexual abuse involves forcing or enticing a child or young person to take part in sexual activities, including prostitution, whether or not the child is aware of what is happening. The activities may involve physical contact, including penetrative (e.g. rape, buggery or oral sex) or non-penetrative acts. They may include non-contact activities, such as involving children in looking at, or in the production of, pornographic material or watching sexual activities, or encouraging children to behave in sexually inappropriate ways.

Neglect

1.31   Neglect is the persistent failure to meet a child's basic physical and/or psychological needs, likely to result in the serious impairment of the child's health or development. Neglect may occur during pregnancy as a result of maternal substance abuse. Once a child is born, neglect may involve a parent or carer failing to provide adequate food or clothing, shelter including exclusion from home or abandonment, failing to protect a child from physical and emotional harm or danger, failure to ensure adequate supervision including the use of inadequate care-takers, or the failure to ensure access to appropriate medical care or treatment. It may also include neglect of, or unresponsiveness to, a child's basic emotional needs.

Running theme: anti-discriminatory practice

In working with families from other ethnicities, practitioners need knowledge of that culture's child-rearing practices, family structure, sex roles, religious beliefs, etc. They should use such information cautiously with an assumption that such information is only a generalisation and should not be used as a stereotype. Efforts to avoid misinterpretation can, ironically, lead to mistakes when practitioners become hesitant to criticise any parenting action, fearing it might be seen as discriminatory whereas, even within the family's ethnic group, it would be seen as harmful.

Racist prejudices, particularly about the violence of black people, have adversely affected people's assessments of families. There is an over-representation of black children in public care, and evidence that they come into care more quickly while black parents are less likely to be offered family support services (Barn, 1990; Chand, 2000).

Racist prejudices can influence judgements in an unconscious way, as illustrated by Birchall and Hallett's (1995) study of practitioners' assessments. They gave a vignette of a referral to a sample of 170 professionals from the main groups involved in child protection work and asked them to make an assessment, based on the information in the vignette. For half the sample, the family's ethnicity was not mentioned while, for the other half, the family was described as Afro-Caribbean; all other details remained the same. There were significant differences in the assessments between the two groups, with more of those for whom the family was described as Afro-Caribbean classifying the case as a child abuse issue (56.5 per cent against 37.9 per cent of the other group) and being less likely to suggest offering help (20 per cent against 31 per cent of the other group).

The NSPCC provides a useful reading list on black and ethnic minority children, young people and families, that can be consulted when dealing with a particular issue. Available from NSPCC Library and Information Service, www.nspcc.org.uk.

The definitions provided by the WHO and *Working Together* are useful but are at a level of generality, however, that leaves a great deal of work to be done in actually applying them in practice and deciding that a child is being abused or neglected. As the later sections of this book show, there are several complexities in applying the definitions in practice:

- *Thresholds*: all parents fall short of perfection at some times. In practice, as discussed in later sections, decisions about thresholds are major dilemmas that professionals are continually having to face. What is 'good enough' parenting and at what point should it cause some concern? Of particular significance in UK law is 'at what point should it be classified as causing or being likely to cause significant harm?' These thresholds are linked to decisions about actions, about offering help or, in more serious cases, taking a more coercive approach. Chronicity and severity are two key factors that influence the decisions.
- *Diversity of parenting and caring styles*: the UK is a multi-cultural society and culture has a major influence on parenting styles so, when working with a family of a particular ethnic group, practitioners need to research the normal customs of that group and assess the family within that framework. Diversity, however, is even more of a complicating factor: it is not just found in different ethnic groups but, even within one group, there is considerable diversity at the micro level of family life that we are dealing with, for example in how children are disciplined, how affection is shown, whether nudity is acceptable or embarrassing.
- *Ambiguity of the evidence*: professionals are not often direct witnesses of actions which are indisputably abusive, and there are few signs or symptoms that are clearly evidence of abuse. The judgement usually has to be made on the basis of indirect and ambiguous evidence so that it contains some degree of uncertainty.
- *Culpability*: it is widely accepted that abuse and neglect have 'multi-factorial' causes. If many different social and individual factors play a part in the causal pathway that leads to the abuse, to what extent is the abuser culpable for the harm done? This raises difficult ethical questions about when we consider individuals to be responsible for their actions and when we consider there are extenuating circumstances that mitigate their guilt. The definition of abuse in the *Core Curriculum of Knowledge and Skills* (DfES, 2005) differs from the definition in the *Working Together* guidance and includes the phrase, 'deliberate act of ill-treatment'. This is similar to the phrases in the WHO definitions

qualifying abusive actions as 'reasonably within the control of ...' or using resources 'reasonably available' to the parent(s). These definitions reflect how judgements about abuse need to be made within a specific social context and giving due weight to the parent's ability to avoid the abuse. It would be offensive to call parents in a famine area 'abusive' because they were unable to provide basic nutrition to their children whereas it would be abusive if affluent parents in England failed to give sufficient food to their children. But where are the boundaries between reasonable and unreasonable behaviour? Parents suffering from mental disorders raise complex questions about judging what it is 'reasonable' to expect of them. What if you were dealing with a family where the mother was failing to meet the child's emotional needs because she was severely depressed? Is her behaviour 'reasonably' within her control?

> For parents, the issue of culpability can be crucial since they may feel unfairly blamed for problems in their child when, in their view, they are doing all that they can, but factors outside their control are interfering with their efforts.

- Actual harm and potential harm: some abuse or neglect has quickly observable consequences – a blow to the head may start a cerebral bleed. Some types, however, feed into a slower process so that the harm may not show itself until later in a child's life. Defining phrases such as 'potential harm' or 'likely to cause significant harm' require professionals to make a prediction about the possible future effects. Although one can understand why predictions are necessary, they present a challenge because of our limited knowledge of how particular experiences will affect particular children. Scientific research on the effects of different child-rearing practices gives us some answers but these are at a general level and do not solve all the dilemmas you face in practice when deciding whether to consider a specific action abusive or not. This is particularly difficult with emotional abuse and neglect where we know that a chronic experience of such treatment can have devastating long-term effects on a child's sense of self-worth and ability to form relationships but, for a particular child receiving a particular pattern of care, how much harm do we speculate will be done?

How common is abuse?

Accurate statistics on incidence are hard to gather because (a) definitions vary so that studies may not be looking at the same phenomena (this makes international comparisons particularly difficult); (b) definitions used in a study are imprecise so people may not always classify the same incident as abusive; (c) for different reasons, both victims and perpetrators may be reluctant to provide honest answers to researchers.

Creighton (2004) provides a useful review of statistics, reflecting the complexity of collecting them by breaking the figures down into layers:

- Layer 1: Those children whose abuse is recorded in the criminal statistics of the country. During the year 1 April 2002 to 31 March 2003, there were 4,109 reported offences of '*cruelty to or neglect of children*' and 1,880 of '*gross indecency with a child under the age of 14*' in England and Wales.
- Layer 2: Those children who are officially recorded as being in need of protection from abuse, e.g. children on Child Protection Registers in England and Wales. There were 30,200 children's names added to the child protection register in England during the same year.
- Layer 3: Those children who have been reported to child protection agencies by the general public, or other professionals such as teachers or doctors, but not registered. There were 570,220 referrals concerning child maltreatment to social services departments, also in 2002–3.
- Layer 4: Abused or neglected children who are recognised as such by relatives or neighbours, but are not reported to any professional agency.
- Layer 5: Those children who have not been recognised as abused or neglected by anyone, including the victims and perpetrators.

Layers 4 and 5 are harder to estimate but some evidence is provided by Cawson et al.'s (2000) study of a random sample of 2,869 18–24-year-olds to explore their childhood experiences of all forms of abuse. Their findings suggest that the majority of victims of abuse are not known to the child protection system. Their results are as follows:

Physical abuse

They defined three levels of severity: (i) serious abuse where there had been violent treatment regularly over the years, or violence which caused physical injury, or frequently led to physical effects lasting at least until the next day; (ii) intermediate abuse where violent treatment occurred irregularly and with less frequent lasting physical effects, or where other physical treatment/discipline such as slaps, smacks and pinches occurred regularly and caused injury or regularly had lasting physical effects; (iii) this level reflected 'cause for concern' where less serious physical treatment/discipline occurred regularly, or where irregular physical discipline often had lasting effects. Occasional slaps, smacks or pinches which rarely or never had lasting effect were excluded from the assessment of abuse.

The researchers classified the responses from young people as showing:

(i)   7% serious abuse
(ii) 14% intermediate abuse
(iii) 3% cause for concern

More girls experienced serious abuse and more boys intermediate abuse. For serious abuse, there was a strong link with social grades D and E, but this trend was not found for other categories.

Physical neglect

This was defined in terms of absence of adequate parental care and supervision, with the two aspects being measured separately.

(i)   6% serious absence of care: e.g. frequently going hungry, going to school in dirty clothes, being abandoned or deserted, living in dangerous physical conditions
(ii) 9% intermediate absence of care: e.g. similar conditions to serious but less frequent
(iii) 2% 'cause for concern': e.g. homes unclean, sometimes no clean clothes for school, rare dental check-ups

For absence of supervision, the figures are:

(i)   5% serious: e.g. allowed to stay at home overnight unsupervised under the age of 10, or allowed to be absent without parents knowing their whereabouts under the age of 14
(ii) 12% intermediate: e.g. left unsupervised at night age 10–11, under-12s frequently left in charge of younger siblings
(iii) 3% cause for concern: e.g. left without adult supervision in the evenings, under the age of 10 going to town centre without an adult or older child

Surprisingly, there were relatively few distinctions by socio-economic grade, given the known association between neglect and poverty.

Emotional or psychological maltreatment

The study measured incidence on seven dimensions:

(i)   34% terrorising
(ii) 24% psychological control and domination
(iii) proxy attacks by harming someone or something a child loves, e.g. attacking their treasured possession (9%) or frequent violence between their carers (5%)

(iv) 18% humiliation/degradation
(v) 17% physical control and domination
(vi) 10% withdrawal
(vii) 10% antipathy

Sexual abuse

There is controversy over the question of the age at which a child can give informed consent to sexual activity. In this study, abuse was measured by asking whether respondents had experienced a range of behaviours under the age of 16. Those under 12 and those who had not consented were both classed as abused; those aged 13–15 when consensual activity took place were included as a borderline 'at-risk' group. One per cent had been abused by parents/carers, almost all including physical contact; 3 per cent abused by other relatives, with 2 per cent contact and 1 per cent non-contact; 11 per cent had been abused by other known people, with 8 per cent contact and 3 per cent non-contact; 4 per cent abused by strangers, with 2 per cent contact and 2 per cent non-contact.

The 'at-risk' group were primarily involved with known non-relatives and comprised 5 per cent of the sample. Women were more likely than men to have experienced all forms of abuse.

Remember that definitions of abuse and neglect are linked to society's views on what is acceptable and unacceptable. Research has been done to find out what ways of treating children are seen as maltreatment. Cawson et al.'s (2000) study on abuse also elicited their views on child-rearing. The results showed considerable variation in opinions. The Department of Health's (1995) summary of research includes a study of the experiences relating to intimacy and sexual activity of a random sample of children between 4 and 16 who had not been abused.

Everyone has some personal values and views about good and bad parenting. Whether or not they are now a parent, all professionals have had the experience of being a child. Separating personal values from professional roles is hard but needs to be done to ensure families are judged against society's standard of what is acceptable, not the worker's own personal views. Our society tolerates a wide range of family styles, some of which can seem very odd and unfamiliar. Families can be unfairly criticised just because their pattern of behaviour is so different from what is 'normal' to the professional. Professionals need to make difficult judgements about whether parenting behaviour that seems strange or unacceptable to them on a personal level is indeed harmful to the child. It is important to be aware of your own values and opinions so that you can check whether you are over-reacting to a family because of how much they differ from yourself.

Taking it **FURTHER**

Although agreement on definitions of abuse and neglect has been reached at an international level, can these definitions be criticised for reflecting a Eurocentric view of child-rearing? For example, the emphasis, in the definition of emotional abuse, on having a primary attachment figure is seen by some as linked to the concept of a nuclear family and so overlooks the family structures found in some other societies. The initial work on attachment theory was conducted on white, middle-class families in the USA, but later research has indicated that there are significant class and cultural variations in 'normal' patterns of parent–child attachments (Dale, Green and Fellows, 2006: 159). What is the evidence on variations in child-rearing practices? Has most research focused on Eurocentric family patterns? Is there evidence of radically different but apparently successful patterns in child-rearing elsewhere?

Further Reading

On the definition of abuse and neglect:

B. CORBY **(2000)** *Child Abuse: towards a knowledge base, Buckingham: Open University Press.*

Department for Education and Skills (2006) Working Together to Safeguard Children, London: DfES, sections 1.22–1.31.

J. KORBIN **(1991)** *'Cross-cultural perspectives and research directions for the 21st century', Child Abuse and Neglect, 15: 67–77.*

N. PARTON **(1985)** *The Politics of Child Abuse, London: Macmillan.*

On the incidence of abuse:

P. CAWSON, C. WATTAM, S. BROOKER AND G. KELLY **(2000)** *Child Maltreatment in the United Kingdom: a study of the prevalence of child abuse and neglect, London: NSPCC.*

S. CREIGHTON **(2004)** *Prevalence and Incidence of Child Abuse: international comparisons, London: NSPCC Research Department.*

Studies of 'normal' family behaviour:

J. NEWSON AND E. NEWSON **(1965)** *Patterns of Infant Care, London: Pelican.*

M. SMITH AND M. GROCKE **(1995)** *Normal Family Sexuality and Sexual Knowledge in Children, London: Royal College of Psychiatrists/Gorkill Press.*

Studies of the longer-term impact of abuse and neglect:

J. GIBBONS, B. GALLAGHER, C. BELL AND D. GORDON **(1995)** *Development after Physical Abuse in Early Childhood, London: HMSO.*

A. MULLENDER AND R. MORLEY **(1994)** *Children Living with Domestic Violence, London: Whiting & Birch.*

2.7

who abuses and why?

Learning outcomes

This section helps the student to:

- Understand how risk factors are identified and measured.

- Know the current evidence on risk factors.

- Be aware of the range of theories and research on abuse and neglect and the research evidence to support them.

- Understand that many of the common risk factors for parental abuse are also risk factors for poor outcomes for children whether or not parental abuse occurs.

- Appreciate the importance of undertaking a comprehensive assessment of a family's strengths and difficulties so that the professional response can be tailored to their individual needs.

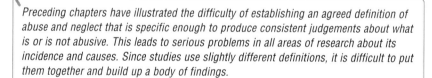

Preceding chapters have illustrated the difficulty of establishing an agreed definition of abuse and neglect that is specific enough to produce consistent judgements about what is or is not abusive. This leads to serious problems in all areas of research about its incidence and causes. Since studies use slightly different definitions, it is difficult to put them together and build up a body of findings.

Researching the causes of abuse

A deeper understanding of the causes of abuse and neglect can help us both to devise better ways of helping abusive families and to predict which families are likely to be abusive, so that efforts can be made to prevent the problem developing. However, progress so far has been modest. There is no known single cause nor does any single description fit all abusive families. Research on abuse takes two main forms:

Studies of correlating factors: one strand of research is to study families and try to identify factors that correlate with abuse. This has produced a body of knowledge about risk factors, that is, characteristics of parents or families that are associated with abuse. It is important to remember that such studies, on their own, only demonstrate a correlation, not a causal relationship. It may be that both the predictive factor and abuse are the result of some other, underlying factor(s). Predictive factors can be used to identify vulnerable groups of families on whom to target preventive or supportive services and, therefore, play a significant role in current policy's aim of providing help at an early stage before problems escalate to a serious level.

Theories of causation: these aim to go beyond correlations to identify the factors that cause the problem and to explain the process by which they cause it. For example, Marziali et al. (2003) theorise that some neglectful parents have a borderline personality disorder because of disturbances in their own childhood and this leads them to have difficulty in maintaining mutually supportive relationships, in regulating their emotions, and in maintaining self-esteem. It is then suggested that this contributes to their observed problems in parenting. Causal explanations generate ideas on how to intervene and either prevent abuse occurring or help abusers change their behaviour.

Understanding risk factors

The goal of risk-factor research is to identify factors that are more common in abusive families than in the rest of the population. Such findings would help professionals predict which families are likely to become abusive. Targeting preventive services on high-risk families is a key strategy in the *Every Child Matters* policy and so this body of research is of great significance.

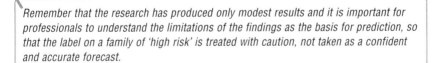

Remember that the research has produced only modest results and it is important for professionals to understand the limitations of the findings as the basis for prediction, so that the label on a family of 'high risk' is treated with caution, not taken as a confident and accurate forecast.

With most predictive instruments in social welfare, *the majority* of those classified as high risk of being abusive are 'false positives', that is, inaccurately classified (Munro, 2004). Therefore, professionals should understand that when a predictive tool is used to identify a high-risk group of families who have not yet abused, although providing some rational basis for targeting resources, all that the research evidence allows us to say is that we expect a higher than average incidence of abuse in families with these characteristics but we do not know which individual families will actually become abusive (or would have done without the professional preventive intervention). Moreover, only a minority of the families will become abusive.

Justice as well as science requires this cautious use of predictions. It is unjust to stigmatise a family on the basis of a faulty understanding of the scientific evidence.

Understanding predictive factors is not straightforward. A risk factor for abuse is something that is found more often in abusive families than in the general population but it is not the frequency alone but the *size of the difference* that determines how strongly it predicts abuse.

Common but weak predictors: something can be very common among abusive families but also fairly common in general so it has little predictive significance. Poverty, for example, is correlated with neglect but, although often (not always) found in neglectful families, it is also found in a large number of non-neglectful families. Indeed, most poor parents are not neglectful. Poverty, however, is correlated with poor outcomes for children independently of parental abuse.

Rare but strong predictors: something can be fairly rare among abusive families yet have strong predictive significance because it is extremely rare in general. The spiral fracture of the arm of a young baby, for example, is a rare sign of abuse but has few other causes and so can trigger a suspicion of abuse (but alternative explanations need to be ruled out).

Unfortunately, the limitations of the research on predictive factors mean that their predictive strength is hard to work out. Different definitions of abuse and different methods of collecting data make it hard to generalise from the various studies. The following illustrates the variability of the findings of risk-factor research: Gelles (1973) found that of 19 psychological traits reported by researchers as predictive of abuse, only 3 were reported by two or more investigators. Similarly, reviews of lists of risk factors used in different states in the USA have reported that the number of factors listed ranged from 5 to 13 and no factor appeared in all risk instruments (Johnson, 1996; Lyons, Doueck and Wodarski, 1996).

There are numerous checklists available that can be used to count the number of factors present in a family but they should be used with caution. They should certainly *not* be used simply to tot up the number of factors present and produce a score for risk level. This would result in a highly unreliable score and be an injustice to the families labelled as dangerous.

Peters and Barlow (2003) reviewed risk instruments designed to predict child abuse during the antenatal and postnatal periods. They report that, at best, only 25 per cent of those identified as high risk were true positives and suggest that such a low percentage reinforces the need to treat a positive result with extreme caution, and certainly not as the basis for any punitive intervention. Their recent warning echoes that made by Dingwall (1989: 51), who reviewed the risk-prediction research and concluded: 'The amount of scientifically validated research on child abuse and neglect is vanishingly small. The value of any self-styled predictive checklist is negligible.'

Sidebotham (2003: 41) provides a good, simple illustration of the limitations of predictive factors:

> In a longitudinal study of children in Avon, one of the strongest identified risk factors for maltreatment was a father who had been in local authority care. For such fathers, the risk of a child being abused was increased six fold. However, of the 169 children whose fathers had been in care, 162 (96 per cent) were not abused.

Hagall (1998) has reviewed the research evidence and produced a list of risk factors for violence which takes account of the strength of the evidence.

Perpetrator-based risk indicators for dangerousness

Factors where research evidence is fairly clear that the risks for violence, at least, are increased:

- a record of previous violence
- level of previous offending of any type
- being male
- having a history of past mental health problems particularly if hospitalised
- personality disorder
- non-compliance (particularly with medication)
- personal history of abuse or neglect
- cognitive distortions concerning the use of violence.

Factors where research evidence is equivocal or insufficient:

- use and availability of weapons
- substance abuse
- current psychiatric symptomatology
- misperceptions about child behaviour.

In no case is the relationship absolute, or the mediator and mechanisms clear.

Victim and situational risk factors

Risk factors relating to the victim:

- being young (under 5, particularly)
- being premature, or of low birthweight
- being more difficult to control
- giving an account of harm or danger.

Risk factors associated with the situation:

- family problems
- low levels of social support
- high levels of socioeconomic stress
- access to the child
- organisational dangerousness and poor decision making.

(Hagall, 1998: 57, 66)

Some factors which look like plausible contributors to abuse have been found in controlled trials *not* to vary between abusive and non-abusive families, that is, to have no predictive value. These are:

- The number (as opposed to the perceptions) of stressful events.
- Self-expressed emotional needs, for example, feeling unloved or showing dependency, emotional problems, or personal adjustment problems.
- Denial of problems. (Wolfe, 1999: 63)

Why does abuse happen?

There is no shortage of theories about the causes of abuse, but although many have some research evidence to support them, no one theory provides a complete explanation of abuse: no one description of an abusive family fits all. Some consensus is emerging in the theoretical literature:

1 Abuse is thought to be multi-factorial, that is, due to the interplay of many factors in many different aspects of family life.

2 Assessment of families needs to cover their strengths as well as their weaknesses (note how this is emphasised in the Common Assessment Framework and the Assessment of Need documents).

3 The causal pathway is dynamic with risk factors interacting with resiliency factors in a particular family, which explains why precise prediction has proved an elusive goal.

4 Small differences in families can lead to big differences in outcomes for children.

Socio-cultural theories

Cultural explanations: In many ways, violence is celebrated in our culture. Movies, cartoons and sporting events all portray violence as an acceptable way of showing one's feelings (Strauss and Gelles, 1990). Moreover, physical chastisement has long been an acceptable way of disciplining a child, legitimating the use of violence towards children. Feminist theorists highlight how society condones male violence in particular and endorses a power imbalance between fathers and their female partners and children (Dobash and Dobash, 1979 and 1987; Yllo, 1993). A related argument is that society offers little deterrence to violence within the home, so that when a father claims that he 'just lost control', he is influenced by the private nature of the family and the low risk of public punishment. It is important to remember that people are far less likely to lose control when there is a severe penalty for doing so (Gelles and Strauss, 1988).

Social stress theories: Poverty, unemployment, poor housing, violent communities and isolation can cause frustration and stress in individuals, making them more likely to vent their feelings in violence (Gelles and Cornell, 1990). This is supported by the correlation between these adverse factors and some forms of abuse (e.g. neglect) but does not explain the incidence of abuse among more affluent and socially included families.

Strain theory: Argues that deviant behaviour is common in societies that value and promise financial success but do not provide equal opportunities. Those who find their path to success blocked become strained and frustrated and are more likely to turn to deviant behaviour such as abusing their children (Merton, 1938).

Biological

A number of studies have reported biological contributions to abuse. Milner and Chilamkurti (1991) found that physical abusers showed a hyper-responsive physiological response to both positive and negative child stimuli. This might make them more physiologically aroused in a stressful situation with a child and so contribute to abuse. Langevin (1993) reported that perpetrators of child sexual abuse had different hormonal levels from comparison groups. Neurological problems, attention deficit disorder, low IQ, physical disability, and physical ill-health have been associated with abuse (Crittendon, 1998; Elliott, 1988; Milner, 1998).

Psychological

Attachment theory: Parents who had poor or insecure attachments to their prime carer in childhood are prone to anxiety, low self-esteem, and an inability to form secure attachments to their own children when they become parents (Bowlby, 1979). This has serious consequences for their children's emotional development, with a risk of perpetuating the problem. It also makes the parents more likely to be abusive or neglectful (Howe, 2005).

Cognitive-behavioural: Using controlled trials to compare the behaviour, thoughts and feelings of abusive parents with other parents, the following differences were identified:

- Low frustration tolerance and inappropriate expressions of anger (as measured by emotional reactivity to provocative child stimuli).
- Social isolation from important sources of support.
- Impaired parenting skills, such as inconsistent, unstimulating, and inflexible approaches to child rearing.
- Unrealistic expectations of their children.
- Subjective parental reports that their child's behaviour is very stressful.
- Descriptions of themselves as inadequate or incompetent in their role as parents.
 (Wolfe, 1999: 64)

Social learning theory: Children learn social and cognitive behaviours by modelling themselves on others, especially those in closest contact, such as parents (Bandura, 1971; Smith and Rachman, 1984). If their childhood experience exposes them to family violence then they learn that violence is an acceptable way, or indeed even *the* acceptable way, of expressing emotions and dealing with conflicts.

This theory is supported by the finding that victims of abuse are more likely than average to become abusers as adults (Strauss et al., 1980; Egeland, 1993). It is essential to remember however that childhood abuse is neither a necessary nor a sufficient condition for becoming an abuser. The *majority* of abused children do *not* become abusive adults (Kaufman and Zigler, 1987; Widom, 1989). See Buchanan, 1996, chapter 2 for a detailed account of inter-generational transmission of abuse. She concludes that there is a growing consensus that around a third of abused children will repeat the pattern as parents.

Psychopathology: In some cases, abuse seems to arise from mental illness or personality disorder in the parent. A small number of severely depressed mothers, for example, kill or injure their babies and their action seems the result of their depressive thinking. Personality disorders arising from disturbed childhood experiences, especially from a lack of security and affection, have been implicated in some forms of neglect (Marziali, Damianakis and Trocme 2003). The literature supports the finding that fewer than 10 per cent of abusers suffer from a major mental illness (Williams and Finkelhor, 1990; Wolfe, 1985). However, a higher number suffer from learning and intellectual deficits and personality disorders (Wolfe, 1985).

Ecological

This approach takes the view that human behaviour should be studied in its full, multi-dimensional context. Sociological, psychological and biological factors all play a part in the causation of abuse. Child abuse is not seen as an isolated incident or just due to defects in the parents, but as 'a symptom of a society that condones the use of violent methods toward family members in certain circumstances, that does not provide adequate services and basic needs for all its members, and that chooses to define maltreatment in relative rather than absolute terms' (Wolfe, 1999: 66).

It is this ecological approach that seems to underpin the current *Every Child Matters* policy, with the government taking a multi-dimensional approach; there are policies to eradicate child poverty, to improve the safety of neighbourhoods, improve housing estates, improve schools, improve parenting skills, and improve professional support to families. The overriding aim is 'to ensure every child has the chance to fulfil their potential' (*Every Child Matters*, 2003) and to reduce all adverse factors in a child's life, not just the harmful effects of abuse and neglect. However, if measures to reduce these factors are successful, then there should also be a reduction in the incidence of parental abuse and neglect since fewer parents will find themselves in the stressful situation where abusive reactions to their children are more likely.

Taking it **FURTHER**

If we accept that abuse and neglect occur because of the interplay of social and personal factors, what are the implications for allocating responsibility or for prioritising where to target change? Has the UK tended to focus on the part played by parents without fully acknowledging that political policies in recent decades have increased inequalities and created many of the conditions that make abuse and neglect more likely? What alternative approaches might be taken? Does the *Every Child Mattters* agenda seek to redress the balance? See Parton (2005) for an interesting discussion of the social construction of child protection services.

Further Reading

K. BROWNE, C. DAVIES, AND P. STRATTON (EDS) (2002) *Early Prediction and Prevention of Child Abuse, Chichester: Wiley. An interesting collection of chapters on difficulties and achievements in predicting and preventing abuse.*

A. BUCHANAN (1996) *Cycles of Child Maltreatment: facts, fallacies and interventions, Chichester: Wiley. A thorough review of the research evidence on the inter-generational transmission of abuse.*

H. CLEAVER, I. UNELL AND J. ALDGATE (1999) *Children's Needs – Parenting Capacity: the impact of parental mental illness, problem alcohol and drug use, and domestic violence on children's development, London: HMSO.*

D. HOWE (2005) *Child Abuse and Neglect: attachment, development, and intervention, Basingstoke: Palgrave Macmillan. A good account of attachment theory with the implications for assessment and intervention well spelled out.*

E. MUNRO (2004) *'A simpler way to understand the results of risk assessment instruments', Children and Youth Services Review, 269: 877–83. Explains the probability theory underlying the interpretation of results, using child abuse instruments as the example.*

D. WOLFE (1999) *Child Abuse: implications for child development and psychopathology, London: Sage Publications. The research evidence on causation is well reviewed and the ecological approach carefully explained.*

2.8

emotional abuse

Learning outcomes

This section will help you understand:

* The processes involved in emotional abuse.

* How the abuse is apparent in the behaviour of the child.

* How the abuse can be assessed in the parent–child interaction.

* The type of parents who are emotionally abusive and its impact on the professional's relationship with the family.

* Factors in the child associated with resilience.

The next four sections cover the evidence, the signs and symptoms, that raise the suspicion that a child is being abused or neglected. The material is organised in the four categories of abuse listed in *Working Together*: emotional abuse, neglect, physical abuse and sexual abuse. I have placed emotional (also known as psychological) abuse first because it is, to some degree, always present in any other form of abuse. Research also suggests that the most common and lasting damaging effects of physical abuse, sexual abuse and neglect are embedded in the emotional abuse experienced (Hart et al., 2002; McGee and Wolfe, 1991). Children may recover from physical pain and injuries but may never recover from the terror, degradation, humiliation, or breach of trust involved (Briggs and Hawkins, 1996). It can cause harmful long-term effects on children's health and development, damaging their capacity for forming successful relationships (Howe, 2005), but there is also evidence to suggest that some children are more resilient at withstanding the impact (Iwaniec, Larkin and Higgins, 2006).

Emotional abuse can occur on its own, although it is used as the main category on child protection registers in less than 20 per cent of cases. It is notoriously hard to prove and, for any legal action, expert assessments of parent–child interactions by child psychologists or psychiatrists are usually obtained.

Definition

In Section 2.6 a general definition of emotional abuse was given, but many efforts have been made to amplify it. Garbarino, Gutterman and Seeley (1986) try to summarise the mechanism at work: 'psychological abuse is a concerted attack by an adult on a child's development of self and social competence, a pattern of psychically destructive behaviour.' They list five key behaviours: rejecting, isolating, terrorising, ignoring and corrupting children.

Monteleone and Brodeur (1998: 372) offer a more detailed list:

1. **Ignoring** the child and failing to provide necessary stimulation, responsiveness, and validation of the child's worth in normal family routine.
2. **Rejecting** the child's value, needs, and requests for adult validation and nurturance.
3. **Isolating** the child from the family and community, denying the child normal human contact.
4. **Terrorising** the child with continual verbal assaults, creating a climate of fear, hostility and anxiety, thus preventing the child from gaining feelings of safety and security.

5. **Corrupting** the child by encouraging and reinforcing destructive, anti-social behaviour until the child is so impaired in socio-emotional development that interaction in normal social environments is not possible.

6. **Verbally assaulting** the child with constant name-calling, harsh threats, and sarcastic put-downs that continually 'beat down' the child's self-esteem with humiliation.

7. **Overpressuring** the child with subtle but consistent pressure to grow up fast and to achieve too early in the areas of academic work, physical/motor skills, and social interaction, which leaves the child feeling that he or she is never quite good enough.

Domestic violence

In addition, exposure to domestic violence between adults is a form of emotional abuse. Brain research has demonstrated changes in the brain functioning of young children exposed to domestic violence that result in different processing of information in the brain. Exposure to domestic violence can lead to symptoms consistent with post-traumatic stress disorder, for example emotional numbing, increased arousal, avoidance of any reminders of the violent event, or obsessive focus on it, depression, and/or violent, behaviour (Giardino and Giardino, 2002: 75). Parkinson and Humphries (1998) also studied the impact of witnessing family violence, and report that the children show higher levels of anxiety, low self-esteem, depression, and particularly poor social competence, such as aggressive behaviour and engagement in fewer social activities. Parents sometimes deny that the child is aware of the violence but most children have some knowledge of what is going on and suffer a reaction.

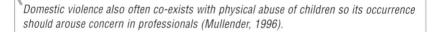

Domestic violence also often co-exists with physical abuse of children so its occurrence should arouse concern in professionals (Mullender, 1996).

Identification

Much abuse takes place in private but emotional abuse is often directly observable by the worker or others in the child's life and assessment is predominantly based on observations of parent–child interactions. The advantages of this visibility, though, are offset by the problems of establishing that the behaviour amounts to emotional abuse. Most parents are insensitive or bad-tempered at times but it is compensated for by a generally loving relationship. Accurate assessment of abuse depends on systematic and rigorous collection of observations over a significant period, preferably in a number of different settings. It is the *pattern* of behaviour that needs to be established. It is only very rarely that a judgement of emotional abuse might be made on the basis of a single incident, something as extreme perhaps as telling a child he was responsible for his mother's suicide attempt.

The *chronicity* of the problem also needs to be checked even when there is clearly an abusive pattern of behaviour at present. Has there been some recent event in the family, such as the death of one parent, that is making the remaining parent insensitive to the child's needs for a time?

> *Scapegoating can occur, where one child is singled out for abusive treatment but the siblings receive an adequate level of care. Therefore, assessment needs to look at the experience of each child individually.*

> *The living circumstances also need to be taken into consideration when assessing emotional abuse. Some families who have recently immigrated may ask children to take on more adult roles than is usual in the UK but, although undesirable, these may be necessary for the economic and practical survival of the family unit. The reality of the environment in which they are living must be taken into account in judging parental behaviour.*

Signs in the child

Failure to thrive is sometimes seen in extreme cases of emotionally abused infants. There are many organic causes of poor growth so the infant needs a thorough medical examination to rule out other causes (Iwaniec, 2004).

Emotional abuse becomes more visible the older a child gets, not because it does not occur in infancy but because its impact on the child's development becomes more apparent. While the child's behaviour can arouse the suspicion that emotional abuse has occurred, it is ambiguous. There are no signs that are specific to emotional abuse; children may act in a variety of ways when with the abusive parent. Some show fear, others are wary, while others may appear indifferent. They may also show their distress more generally in a variety of ways, such as indiscriminate attachment to others, aggressive behaviour, frozen watchfulness, anxiety, low self-confidence, withdrawal. All of these may have other causes and are not specific to emotional abuse. Their presence, however, should trigger questions about why they are behaving in this way, and one possibility for exploration is that of emotional abuse.

The official guidance on assessment of the child's problems (Department of Health, 2003: 36) recommends using the Strengths and Difficulties Questionnaires developed by Goodman (1997) and Goodman, Meltzer and Bailey (1998). These scales are a modification of Michael Rutter's instruments to screen for emotional and behavioural problems in children and adolescents. They incorporate five scales: pro-social, hyperactivity, emotional problems, conduct (behavioural) problems, and peer problems. They are available in 40 languages on the following website: http://www.sdqinfo.com.

Running theme: the voice of the child

Remember the importance of talking to the child. Research repeatedly finds that, all too often, children are not fully recognised as active participants or as a valuable source of information (Gough, 1997).

Observation and reports of parent–child interactions

The main source of evidence of emotional abuse is from observations of the parent and child together – either the worker's own observations, or reports from others on what they have seen.

In assessing the level of abuse in the parent–child interaction, useful questions are:

How intense is the adverse behaviour?
How much does it dominate/pervade the relationship?
How varied is the behaviour; how many forms have you seen?
Are there others in the child's life with whom there is a good relationship to provide some counterbalance to the abuse?
What are the child's developmental needs at his/her age and how might the abuse affect them?

Remember the importance of working with other professionals: good communication between those who know the family greatly improves accurate identification of emotional abuse. Since different professionals see the parent–child interactions in different contexts, their shared perceptions build up a multi-dimensional picture of the extent of the abuse.

Characteristics of victims

In general, there are no specific characteristics of the children who become the victims of emotional abuse in terms of their gender, age, ordinal position in the family, or health status (Iwaniec, Larkin and Higgins, 2006). One exception is that children with physical or intellectual disabilities are more vulnerable. Children with registered disabilities were found to be up to three times more likely to experience emotional abuse than those without (Sullivan and Knutson, 2000).

Characteristics of abusers

Giardino and Giardino (2002: 84) summarise the research findings on emotionally abusive parents. As a group, some characteristics are common, but non-abusive parents can also have some of these characteristics, so they are not decisive evidence. Moreover, emotional abuse can occur in families which do not seem to contain any of these risk factors:

    emotionally abused as a child
    stressed
    lack of appropriate coping skills
    mental illness
    angry/hostile
    ambivalent towards parenthood
    few resources (financial or social)
    inappropriate expectations of children
    lack of knowledge of normal child development
    marital problems
    lack of impulse control
    substance misuse
    perpetrates domestic violence or lets child live in violent home.

Parental behaviour to professionals

Many parents who emotionally abuse have had disturbed childhood experiences themselves so that they are ill-prepared for meeting the emotional needs of their children. Howe (2005) uses attachment theory to analyse the mechanisms at work in producing the abusive behaviour. A history of disturbed attachment in their own childhoods makes them react with anxiety and agitation when they meet their child's need for attachment to them. 'Defensively, they deal with their anxiety by "deactivating" their caregiving. They therefore fail to provide care and protection at the very moment their child needs it' (2005: 92). He describes how their attachment problems may affect their relationships with professionals:

> Often polite, but wary and distant at first, carers either become disengaged from professional help, or react aggressively, threateningly and with intimidation. ... Professionals are diverted from seeing the child.

He warns that professionals working with such parents can themselves feel intimidated:

> Initially, while the parent is weighing up the professional, interaction might be conducted in a cool but polite fashion. The parent is keen to know the reasons for the involvement. Feeling most safe when they are on top of the rules of engagement, carers might become very knowledgeable about the legislation that underpins the practitioner's work. ... The parent's wish is to keep childcare authorities out of his or her life. Health and welfare workers evoke caregiving and attachment issues that will be dealt with defensively using highly dismissive strategies. ... Most professionals feel a degree of anxiety and stress working with such difficult and intimidating parents. (Howe, 2005: 98)

> As with so much of the evidence in child protection work, this reaction to professionals is ambiguous – it can also be displayed by innocent parents who have been wrongly accused of abuse.

Taking it **FURTHER**

Emotional abuse is said to present particular challenges to children's services because the perpetrators are often acting out the damage they received in their childhoods and need skilled therapeutic help to change. Even if available, this takes time, and the child's immediate needs have to be considered. How can you balance the child's immediate care needs and the parent's longer-term therapeutic needs? Can you argue that your professional duty is to the child not the parent? What are the possible consequences, both good and bad, of separating the parent and child (consider their age, available family support, local foster and adoptive resources). Can you find ways of meeting the child's needs without removing them from the parent?

Further Reading

On identifying and assessing emotional abuse:

A. GIARDINO AND E. GIARDINO (2002) *Recognition of Child Abuse for the Mandated Reporter*, St Louis, MI: G.W. Medical Publishing, Inc. Chapter 5 is on psychological abuse.

D. GLASER (2002) 'Emotional abuse and neglect (psychological maltreatment): a conceptual framework', *Child Abuse and Neglect*, 26: 697–714.

D. HOWE (2005) *Child Abuse and Neglect: attachment, development and intervention*, Basingstoke: Palgrave Macmillan. All of this book is worth reading for an understanding of the significance of attachment theory to understanding children and families, but chapter 6 is specifically on psychological maltreatment.

D. IWANIEC (1995) *The Emotionally Abused and Neglected Child: identification, assessment, and intervention*, Chichester: John Wiley.

D. IWANIEC, E. LARKIN AND S. HIGGINS (2006) 'Research review: risk and resilience in cases of emotional abuse', *Child and Family Social Work*, 11: 73–82.

P. SULLIVAN AND J. KNUTSON (2000) 'Maltreatment and disabilities: a population-based epidemiological study', *Child Abuse and Neglect*, 24: 1257–74.

On failure to thrive:

D. IWANIEC (2004) *Children Who Fail to Thrive: a practice guide*, Chichester: Wiley.

On domestic violence:

A. MULLENDER (1996) *Rethinking Domestic Violence: the social work and probation response*, London: Routledge.

2.9	
neglect	

Learning outcomes

This section will help you understand:

- The problems in reaching a judgement that a child is experiencing neglect.
- Factors to consider in reaching that judgement.

- The importance of a thorough assessment and good recording so that an accurate picture can be gained and progress can be monitored.

- The characteristics of neglectful parents.

Definition

Moving from a general definition of neglect such as that in *Working Together to Safeguard Children* (DfES, 2006b) to more precise definitions is complex. In practice, account has to be taken of local cultural beliefs and values about good-enough parenting and local levels of resources – of what standard of care is generally feasible.

Issues in defining neglect:

1 *Dimensions of neglect*: neglect can be shown in failure to provide an adequate level of care and supervision in any dimension of a child's life. The *Framework for the Assessment of Children in Need and their Families* (Department of Health, 2000) covers seven elements of child development and provides a useful framework for considering neglect. Knowledge about child development and about cultural beliefs and values offers some guidance in defining what counts as neglect.

2 *Level of severity*: the major problem in making the definition more precise is in stating how much below the average the care needs to be before it becomes neglect. It is difficult to decide how far parents can deviate from the norm before society intervenes. However, severity should not be judged solely on the level of neglect present at one particular time. Its adverse impact on children's health and development is significantly related to its chronicity. Therefore, assessments of severity need to consider both how bad the neglect is and how long the child has been exposed to it.

3 *Lowering standards*: you might expect that professionals could be guilty of imposing their own values on lower-income service users but, oddly enough, research shows that they tend to have lower expectations than the families themselves. It seems that they see so many poorly functioning families that they alter their expectations. In America, Rose and Meezan (1996) compared views on neglect of mothers on low incomes and social workers, and found that the mothers thought neglect was much more serious that the social workers did. They also found mothers from ethnic minorities had higher standards than native white Americans.

4 *Assigning responsibility*: the problem of assigning responsibility is particularly acute with the neglect which is due to in adverse social circumstances, raising questions about the degree of responsibility the parents have for the neglect. The issue is complicated by professionals' emotional responses to neglectful parents. Allsop and Stevenson (1995) found that social workers often felt compassion for the parents, especially the mothers, and this made them reluctant to describe their actions as neglectful. Gough (2003: 42) raises three challenging questions:

Should definitions of neglect:

- only apply to direct intentional lack of care or also apply to lack of care due to parental poverty, physical illness or mental illness?
- apply to harm caused by observance of religious or other beliefs where the parents are concerned that health care (such as blood transfusions) or lack of certain ritualistic acts (such as circumcision) may cause greater harm to the child?
- apply equally to lack of care caused by circumstances within or not within the carer's control? If so, then to what extent are carers responsible for lack of care due to substance abuse, or relationship conflict and separation?

The impact of neglect is still harmful and the child needs help, whatever conclusion is reached about the parents' degree of responsibility.

In practice, finding agreement on definitions of neglect is problematic. Horwath's (2003: 73) study of Irish social workers found the following four factors influenced workers' definitions:

1. the effect of individual beliefs;
2. the influence of the team in establishing working definitions of child neglect;
3. the assessment process: e.g. which family members were consulted about what was happening and why;
4. the use of language – frequent reference was made to 'good enough parenting' but workers meant different things by this.

Stevenson (1998: 1) reminds us of another feature of neglect that conveys something of the damaging impact it has on the child. In neglectful families:

There is usually a sense of social distance from others and an awareness of difference which in turn provokes reactions in the family members and the community within which they are located: in truth, a vicious circle.

Identifying neglect

Instances of neglect fall on a continuum, ranging from minor and short-term to serious and chronic. For professionals, the problems lie in determining what level of neglect warrants what type of intervention. In practice, there are three significantly different thresholds: at the lowest level of neglect, non-social-work professionals may consider that they can deal with the problem. If it is more serious, they may judge that it is necessary to refer the family to the local authority social work team for Section 17 family support help. At the third and higher level, the degree of neglect may warrant the case being treated as a Section 47 child protection case.

Working Together guidance defines neglect as the 'persistent' failure to meet a child's needs likely to result in serious impairment of the child's health or development. The focus on 'persistent' emphasises the importance of keeping detailed and precise records of the level of care and supervision offered so that judgements about severity can be made.

- *Range of evidence*: the presenting problem may be restricted to one dimension of a child's care but it is important to take an overview since one area of neglect raises the possibility of a more widespread problem. The Assessment of Need forms and the Common Asssessment Framework both encourage such a holistic approach. Parents may be able to maintain an adequate standard in the most visible parts of their lives but be seriously neglectful in others.

> *Max Piazzini died in 1980 after coming into care because of neglect and then being returned home. Social workers monitoring his care judged the parents' level of care by the state of the living room, which was kept reasonably clean. Max died in a bedroom that was freezing cold and filthy. (Birmingham City Council, 1980)*

- *Sources of evidence*: If possible, all family members should be interviewed, although, in practice, there is a tendency to focus on mothers. Children and fathers are particularly likely to be overlooked (Horwath, 2003) although both groups have distinctive contributions to make in helping professionals gain a rounded picture of family life.
- *Precision of evidence*: Recording needs to provide specific details of the level of care or supervision and any perceptible effects this appears to be having on the child's health or development.

What is essential is to record baseline details and re-take them as work with the family progresses so that it can be seen whether things are getting better or worse. Progress is likely to be slow and so can be easily missed. Or there might be progress on some very visible things, which misleads professionals into thinking there is general improvement. Professionals who have put a lot of effort into helping a family to improve their functioning tend to want to see progress and so can be blind to evidence that the level of care is unchanging or, even worse, dropping. Also, families often show some immediate improvement while the services are being offered or they are being monitored, but slip back when the professionals reduce contact.

Characteristics of neglectful parents

The social stress theory of abuse is particularly relevant in understanding neglect. Neglect is more strongly correlated with poverty than any other form of abuse (Drake and Pandey, 1996; Crittendon, 1988). Poverty, family size, and being a single-parent family are all interrelated and significantly increase the risk of neglect (Browne and Lynch, 1998). Therefore, the implementation of the *Every Child Matters* agenda should, if successful, have a significant impact on reducing neglect.

Psychological factors in the parents also have a role. These should not be seen as wholly separate from social and economic factors – the causal path by which the latter impact on parenting may be via their psychological impact on the parents. Stress, for instance, can be a causal factor in mental illness and alcohol or substance misuse.

Research on characteristics of neglectful parents has mainly focused on mothers, reflecting the cultural bias towards considering mothers to have primary responsibility for bringing up children, moreover, it is found that there is a higher rate of neglect in lone-parent families.

- Social isolation is common – many parents left their childhood homes as soon as they could to get away from abusive or neglectful parents, so they do not have the wider family support. Coohey (1995) compared neglectful and average mothers. Neglectful mothers were found to have below average contact with their own mothers and partners, were more likely to describe their mothers as not warm or caring, as providing a less positive relationship, and they were less interested in receiving help from mothers. Partners tended to have known each other for a shorter time, were less likely to be living together, and had a lower rate of contact. Neglectful mothers, as opposed to non-neglectful ones, have also been found to report that their neighbours are less supportive (Polansky et al., 1985).

- The young age of the mother at the time of first pregnancy – this is exacerbated by low birthweight or prematurity of the baby (Zuravin and DiBlasio, 1992).
- There is evidence of low educational achievement, low intelligence, and poor problem-solving skills (Zuravin and DiBlasio, 1992; Crittenden, 1988).
- The parents have inappropriate expectations about child development – either too high or too low compared with non-neglectful parents (Twentyman and Plotkin, 1982).
- There may be domestic violence, mental illness, and alcohol or substance abuse (Erickson and Egeland, 1996). (These factors are associated with all forms of abuse and are not specific to neglect.)
- There are several sub-types of neglecting parents: Wilson, Kuebli and Hughes's (2005) study of neglecting caregivers identified five distinct patterns of maternal behaviour with implications for how to intervene – significantly impaired, markedly disinhibited, low-efficacy, positively rated and transitional.

Stevenson (1998: 2) lists four common factors in neglectful families known to Social Services Departments in the UK:

1. Most were in extreme poverty. In a few cases, the cause seemed more related to emotional problems, such as substance abuse, so that they did not attend to the needs of the children. Family circumstances were often described as 'chaotic' and children were unsupervised and under-stimulated. They appeared sad and anxious, often displaying aggression and social withdrawal. The main social work concern was for the children's welfare and quality of life but there was an edge of anxiety about their physical safety (due to being unsupervised or the house not having the usual safety precautions when there are young children around.)
2. The parents were mostly single and female, often with one or more of a range of problems from learning difficulties, physical or mental health problems, alcohol abuse and drug addiction. Almost none was sadistically neglectful.
3. Nearly all the families had a long relationship with social workers, sometimes over three generations.
4. In the majority of cases, the parenting was hovering on the edge of 'not good enough', with families 'bumping along the bottom' until perhaps an incident of physical abuse triggered a more coercive response.

Taking it **FURTHER**

It has been said that neglect is itself a neglected subject and the dominance of other forms of abuse in the literature bears this out. Given the chronicity of neglect problems and their impact on children's development, why might their significance be downplayed by child protection services? Has the way practice has become incident-focused made it less sensitive to detecting long-term abuse or neglect where there is no dramatic event to draw attention to the poor quality of care the child is receiving? Does the difficulty of providing effective help and seeing an enduring and substantial improvement in parenting quality lead professionals to become disheartened about the value of intervening in neglectful families? Does the cost of providing long-term help to shore up neglectful families deter agencies from making a commitment except in extreme cases?

Further Reading

J. JONES AND A. GUPTA **(1998)** *'The context of decision-making in cases of child neglect', Child Abuse Review, 7: 97–110.*

B. MINTY AND G. PATTINSON **(1994)** *'The nature of child neglect', British Journal of Social Work, 24: 733–47. Includes a useful framework for recording the specific evidence of neglect.*

RESEARCH IN PRACTICE **(2005)** *Understanding and Working with Neglect. Darlington Quality Protects Research Briefing No. 10. Available from www.rip.org.uk. A valuable summary of what is currently known about the causes and responses to neglect.*

O. STEVENSON **(1998)** *Neglected Children: issues and dilemmas, Oxford: Blackwell Science. A detailed and compassionate exploration of all aspects of working with neglectful families.*

B. STONE **(1998)** *'Child neglect: practitioners' perspectives', Child Abuse Review, 7: 87–96.*

J. TAYLOR AND B. DANIEL (EDS) **(2003)** *Child Neglect: practice issues for health and social care, London: Jessica Kingsley. A wide-ranging set of chapters, covering theoretical and practice issues. See especially N. Spencer and N. Baldwin, 'Economic, cultural and social contexts of neglect'. This chapter provides an excellent, brief review and discussion of the research evidence on the economic, cultural and social factors correlated with neglect.*

D. WILSON AND W. HORNER **(2005)** *'Chronic child neglect: needed developments in theory and practice', Families in Society: The Journal of Contemporary Social Services, 86 (4): 471–81. www.familiesinsociety.org.*

2.10

physical abuse

Learning outcomes

This section will help you understand:

- The difference between 'reasonable chastisement' and physical abuse.

- The main types of injury that arise from physical abuse.

- The sources of evidence that help you make a judgement that physical abuse has occurred.

- The characteristics of victims.

'Reasonable' physical punishment

Physical abuse can range from minor to major, even fatal, injury. Deciding that some action is abusive is complicated by the fact that some degree of physical chastisement is legal and widely practised in this society. When asked to explain injuries on a child, many parents defend their behaviour on the grounds that they were disciplining their child in an acceptable way.

The Children Act 2004, Section 58, sets out the criteria for differentiating 'reasonable punishment' from abuse. Causing actual or grievous bodily harm (ABH and GBH) to a child is criminal. Injuries which are considered as common assault where the victim is an adult, will be charged as ABH in the case of children, 'although prosecutors must bear in mind that the definition of common assault occasioning actual bodily harm requires the injury to be more than transient and trifling'. These injuries are as follows:

- grazes
- scratches
- abrasions
- minor bruising
- swelling
- superficial cuts
- black eye
- reddening of the skin which stays for hours or days.

Identifying abuse

The three main sources of evidence are: (1) the signs and symptoms of injury; (2) what the child says and does; (3) what the parents say and do.

The signs and symptoms of injury

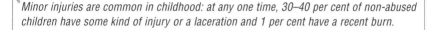

Minor injuries are common in childhood: at any one time, 30–40 per cent of non-abused children have some kind of injury or a laceration and 1 per cent have a recent burn.

Injuries that arouse serious concern: because the following injuries are unlikely to be the result of accidents (although occasionally so), they are therefore highly suggestive of abuse:

- finger-tip bruising
- adult human bite-marks
- cigarette burns
- lash marks
- torn frenulum (the band of tissue linking the middle of the inside top lip to the gum)
- unexplained bleeding in the brain or the retina.

On the whole, though, physical abuse cannot be identified on the basis of a single injury alone but from a combination of factors that, taken together, may produce a pattern that causes concern. It is important to get a detailed account both of the nature of the injury and of its circumstances.

Physical signs that may indicate physical abuse

Bruising   The most common sign of abuse. Based on a review of the research evidence, Maguire et al. (2005) concluded that babies who are not mobile do not usually have any bruises (fewer than 1 per cent), while 17 per cent of infants who are starting to move about, 53 per cent of toddlers and the majority of schoolchildren have bruises. Therefore, it is not usually the simple presence of a bruise that causes concern. Non-accidental bruises can be identified by considering the following factors:

1   Where is the bruise?

Accidental bruises tend to be in places where bone is fairly close to the skin, e.g. forehead, chin, elbows, knees. These are the places that will hit the ground or door in an accidental fall.

Non-accidental bruises are more often on soft tissue sites such as cheeks, mouth, upper leg or around the buttocks or genitalia.

2 What does the bruise look like?

Shape: does it show what type of object caused it? For example, is it the shape of a cigarette, a belt or buckle, a hand or a stick?

Severity: shown by the severity of the injury *or* the number of bruises.

Colour: the colour of a bruise indicates its age and so can be a useful check on the parents' account of what caused the bruise. A rough guide to the colour of bruises is:

red/purple	–	less than 24 hours old
purplish-blue	–	12–48 hours
brown	–	48–72 hours
yellow	–	more than 72 hours.

Several bruises of differing colours indicates several different injuries and this may be a cause for concern.

NB: this is based on white skin.

Bites   Human bite-marks are strong indicators of abuse. In infants, they tend to be around the genitalia or buttocks, often inflicted as punishment. Older children have bites associated with assault or sexual abuse; these are generally multiple, random and well defined. They may be associated with a sucking mark. Young children often bite each other in anger, so ascertaining the size of the bite-mark is important.

Fractures   Diagnosis of a fracture requires medical examination but a fracture may be suspected when there is pain, swelling and discolouration over a bone or joint. The child's age is a significant factor in assessing the cause of fractures. *Accidental* fractures are most common in school-age children, but 94 per cent of *fractures due to abuse* occur in children under 3. Most accidental fractures to babies and toddlers occur from falls. Several fractures of varying ages are suggestive of abuse.

Head injury   This is the major cause of fatal outcome in abuse – estimates range from 40 to 75 per cent of deaths. And even if the child does not die, he or she may be left with serious brain damage. In the first year of life, 95 per cent of serious head injuries have been estimated to be due to abuse, caused by either hitting or shaking (or a combination). However, this hypothesis has come in for severe criticism recently and there is a school of medical opinion that claims there are several other causes of the symptoms besides abuse (Geddes and Plunkett, 2004).

If an infant rolls off a bed or changing table, it is very rare to have much injury. Twenty per cent have a single cut, lump or bruise and only about 1 per cent will have a fracture. Additional concern is felt if there is a lot of bleeding. An exception to this level of injury is if a child falls downstairs with a heavy object like a bike or baby walker. You can usually check this story by looking at the damage done to the staircase.

Burns and scalds   These are found in 10 per cent of abused children (but diagnosis is difficult so they tend to be under-recognised). The peak age for *accidental* burns is during the second year; the peak age for *deliberate* burns is the third year. Repeated accidental burns are rare – most parents and children learn from the one experience because it is so painful.

Any burn with a clear outline is suspicious: cigarette burns; linear burns suggestive of being held against an electric fire; scalds with a clear line where the arm was in the water (in accidents, a child struggles to get out and this causes splash-marks).

Poisoning   *Accidental* poisoning is very common, *non-accidental* poisoning is rare but very serious. One of the commonest forms of abusive poisoning is salt – it leads to drowsiness and seizures and sometimes death. Sometimes poisonous substances may be given as unorthodox medicine but with good intent.

Suffocation   This mostly happens to children under a year old. They present as either cases of sudden death or repeated cases of floppy babies whom the mother says has had some kind of seizure at home. Although the precise number is a matter of continual dispute, most cot deaths are *not* due to abuse (estimates are between 2–10 per cent).

Fabricated or Induced Illness (FII) (previously known as Munchausen Syndrome by Proxy)   This rare, but often serious form of abuse involves the parent (usually the mother; in less than 5 per cent of cases is it the father) fabricating or inducing illness in the child in order to get medical attention. The child may suffer harm directly from the induced symptoms but also indirectly by being subjected to extensive and painful investigations and operations as a result. Sometimes they suffer harm or can even have their life threatened by the efforts of the carer to create symptoms (estimates are 10 per cent die, and most of the rest will suffer from long-term illness). They also suffer unintentional abuse from medical staff in that they are subjected to unnecessary investigations and treatments as a result of the mother's false information.

The existence of cases of Fabricated or Induced Illness has been challenged by some, but persuasive evidence that at least some cases occur was provided by a medical team in Staffordshire who secretly videoed suspected cases when the child was admitted to hospital (Southall et al., 1997). They obtained direct evidence of the parent attempting to suffocate the child. There was also evidence of emotional abuse and physical abuse such as broken bones, in many of the cases. They judged that the parents were suffocating their children to gain attention from doctors, more than to kill the child.

While the existence of F11 is fairly well attested it is undoubtedly the case however, that some families have suffered miscarriages of justice because of wrongful diagnosis.

> *Angela Cannings endured the tragic loss of her two babies and then had the additional horror of being wrongfully convicted of their murders and sent to prison on the basis of a diagnosis of Munchausen Syndrome by Proxy. The Appeal Court rejected the medical evidence for this diagnosis and she was released from prison. The paediatrician who had given the evidence to the court at the original hearing was later struck off the Medical Register for gross professional misconduct but this was overturned on appeal.*

As a result of Angela Cannings' experience and very energetic campaigning by some parent groups and the media (MAMA, 2006) the diagnosis of FII has become fraught, with many professionals feeling apprehensive about getting involved. On the plus side, this public pressure reinforces the need for good evidence before reaching such an extreme diagnosis. In another legal case (High Court of Justice Family Division, 2006, para. 178), where a county council's obtaining of an Emergency Protection Order for a case of FII was found to be at fault, the judge concluded:

> For my part, I would consign the label MSBP to the history books and however useful FII may apparently be to the child protection practitioner I would caution against its use other than as a factual description of a series of incidents or behaviours that should then be accurately set out (and even then only in the hands of the paediatrician or psychiatrist/psychologist). ... What I seek to caution against is the use of the label as a substitute for factual analysis and risk assessment.

On the whole, diagnosis of Fabricated Illness by Proxy is made within a health setting. Doctors or nurses may be concerned about the possibility when:

- Reported symptoms and signs found on examination are not explained by any medical condition from which the child may be suffering.
- Physical examination and results of investigations do not explain symptoms or signs.
- There is an inexplicably poor response to prescribed medication and treatment.
- New symptoms are reported on resolution of previous ones.
- Reported symptoms and signs are not observed in the absence of the carer.
- The child's normal, daily life activities are being curtailed beyond that which might be expected from any known medical disorder from which the child is known to suffer.

> *A sick child arouses anxiety in most parents. Differentiating the appropriate level of anxiety and help-seeking behaviour from the abnormal is problematic. There are illnesses that doctors fail to diagnose or are slow to recognise. Parents can know their child so well that they spot the first signs of trouble before it is apparent to health professionals, so they may disagree with their doctor and be right. If the possible diagnosis of FII is treated as certain, then any action or comment from the parent can be interpreted to support it, potentially leading to gross injustice. The diagnosis should always be treated with caution and other explanations for the child's symptoms looked for.*

What the child says and does

The child's behaviour may change and show any of a range of signs of distress, for example becoming withdrawn, aggressive or anxious. However, there are no signs of distress that are specific to physical abuse nor does the absence of apparent distress rule out abuse.

Getting an honest account of what has happened from children can be difficult because of a combination of fear and loyalty. If a child reports abuse, this should always be taken seriously even if there are no longer any signs of injury. Some may lie to get their parents into trouble but such an explanation should not be readily accepted. If you ask children to explain their injuries in front of the parent who has abused them, common sense tells you they are likely to be scared to tell the truth. However, even taking them to a separate room before asking does not guarantee a truthful answer because they may still fear what may happen when later left alone with the parent.

Observation of the parent–child relationship can be informative – for example some abused children show 'frozen watchfulness' – but absence of fear or wariness does not guarantee an absence of abuse.

Remember the importance of talking to the child. A recurrent finding in inquiries into child deaths is that professionals do not talk to the child. Victoria Climbie was in contact with many doctors, nurses, social workers, but, during the eight months she was in London, no one engaged her in a significant conversation about what was happening to her or how her injuries had arisen.

What the parents say and do

Pointers to non-accidental injury (from Meadows, 1997):

1 There is a delay in seeking medical help (or none is sought).

2 The story of the 'accident' is vague and may vary with repeated telling.

3 The account is not compatible with the injury observed.

4 The parents' affect is abnormal – normal parents are full of creative anxiety for their child, abusive parents tend to be more preoccupied with their own problems, e.g. how soon they can return home.

5 The parents' behaviour gives cause for concern – e.g. they become hostile, rebut accusations that have not been made, avoid seeing the consultant.

6 The child's appearance and his interaction with parents are abnormal, e.g. sad, withdrawn or frightened. Full blown 'frozen watchfulness' is a late stage; its absence does not exclude NAI.

7 The child may say something. Always interview child (if old enough) in privacy. If an out-patient, child may be reluctant to open up as s/he is expecting to be returned to the abusing parents.

Running theme: working with parents

Remember the importance of keeping men in the picture: there is a large body of evidence that shows how child protection work is predominantly carried out with mothers, with men playing a relatively small part despite being on average more violent than women (Mattinson and Sinclair, 1987; Corby, 1987; Farmer and Owen,

1995; Buckley, 2003). Fathers and father figures are frequently not included in information-gathering sessions and assessments of their parenting are consequently often poor, leading to major mistakes in assessing the child's safety. One reason for their absence can be that they pose a greater physical threat to practitioners than women do, and therefore interviewing them is more daunting (Scourfield, 2002). Another factor is that women are assumed to carry the major responsibility for children and so, even when they are not the perpetrators of abuse, they are still seen as the prime protector of the child (Scourfield, 2001).

Long-term impact of physical abuse

Some of the injuries inflicted on children leave permanent damage. The violent shaking of a baby is particularly dangerous in this respect, with a significant risk of permanent brain damage or death (National Institute of Neurological Disorders and Stroke, 2001).

There are psychological consequences too. There is much evidence to suggest that physically abused children are more likely to develop aggressive behaviour problems. They are more likely to interpret their peers as hostile, and to respond inappropriately in an aggressive manner (Dodge, Bates and Petit, 1990) and they are more likely to be involved in family and non-family violence (Malinosky-Rummell and Hansen, 1993).

> *The presence of child physical abuse should make you question whether there is also domestic violence towards a partner.*

Running theme: working with other professionals

Once the suspicion of physical abuse has been raised, you need other professionals who are in contact with the child to be alert to any further evidence of injury and pass the information on to the key worker so that it can be accurately collated. Abusive parents can go to great lengths to conceal signs of injury, such as taking the child to a different Accident and Emergency Department so that the link with previous injuries is harder to spot, or keeping the child away from school until the visible signs have faded.

Characteristics of the victims

Age: the younger a child, the more likely is serious injury or death. A baby can suffer permanent brain damage from being shaken in anger, while an older child can survive unharmed. There is evidence that the number of cases of physical abuse known to child protection services declines with the age of the child (US DHHS, 1998). However, self-reports of abuse indicate no decrease as children get older (Strauss et al., 1998). One possible explanation for this discrepancy is that cases involving more serious injury are referred to child protection services and these occur predominantly in younger children.

Gender: boys seem to be at slightly higher risk than girls (Wolfner and Gelles, 1993).

Disability: children with disabilities are more vulnerable to all forms of abuse than others. The National Center on Child Abuse and Neglect's study estimated that children with disabilities were 1.7 times more likely to be abused (US DHHS, 1993).

 Taking it **FURTHER**

When the Children Act 2004 was going through Parliament, there was a major campaign to include a ban on any form of physical punishment for children. It was argued that children should be given the same protection in law as adults and that permitting physical punishment was an infringement of their human rights. Another argument was that a society that condones the use of physical methods of chastisement increases the likelihood of individual parents going too far and abusing their children. What is the case for saying that a ban would contribute to the reduction of serious physical abuse? Is society's tolerance of some degree of physical punishment a contributory factor to the more dangerous levels of abuse? What can we learn from the evidence from countries such as Sweden that have banned all physical punishment?

Further Reading

CHILD ABUSE AND NEGLECT (2002) *(Special edition on Munchausen by Proxy Syndrome), 26 (5) This set of articles covers a range of issues in defining, identifying and dealing with MSBP, known in the UK as FII.*

B. CORBY (2000) *Child Abuse: towards a knowledge base, 2nd edn, Buckingham: Open University Press. Offers a wide-ranging discussion of research, theories and practice in child protection.*

DEPARTMENT OF HEALTH (2002) *Safeguarding Children in Whom Illness is Fabricated or Induced, London: HMSO, or www.doh.gov.uk. A key reference, offering official guidance on dealing with cases of FII.*

S. MAGUIRE, M. MANN, J. SIBERT. AND A. KEMP (2005) *'Are there patterns of bruising in childhood which are diagnostic or suggestive of abuse? A systematic review', Archives of Diseases in Childhood, 90: 182–6.*

R. MEADOWS (ED.) (1997) *ABC of Child Abuse, London: BMJ Publishing. A medically oriented book, but with relatively little technical language, providing useful summaries of key issues in dealing with abuse.*

K. WILSON AND A. JAMES (2002) *The Child Protection Handbook, 2nd edn, Edinburgh: Bailliere Tindall. Chapter 5, 'The effects of child abuse: signs and symptoms' contains a discussion of the signs and consequences of physical abuse.*

2.11

sexual abuse

Learning outcomes

This section will help you to understand:

- Why society is now more concerned about sexual abuse.

- The three main sources of evidence.

- What is known about which children are likely to be victims.

- What is known about who sexually abuses children.

- What the long-term impact is on the child's development.

Definitions

There are four components in most attempts to define sex abuse:

1   They are broad enough to include abuse inside and outside the family.

2   They include sexual experiences with a child that involve both physical and non-contact activities.

3 They emphasise the exploitation of the child by adult authority and power to achieve the adult's sexual needs, with an implicit assumption that a child cannot give informed consent because he or she does not fully understand what is going on and has so much less power.

4 The perpetrator has an age advantage over the child – and although not necessarily an adult, he or she will be older, bigger or stronger.

Growing social awareness and condemnation of child sexual abuse

Society is much more aware of the incidence of sexual abuse and there is a strong consensus that it is wrong. Factors that have influenced this change are:

- Increased knowledge of how common it is.
- Increased understanding of how much short- and long-term harm it does to a child – an important point when doing a needs assessment.
- Increased concern for the rights of children.
- Challenges to the patriarchal society that saw women and children as the property of men. The increased status of women and children has led to greater condemnation of violence towards them. In the 1970s and 1980s, it was accounts from feminist victims of abuse that helped to shift public opinion on both its prevalence and its damaging effects. The discovery of sexual abuse differed from that of physical abuse, in that it was mainly adults telling of childhood experiences, not adults identifying children as being currently abused. Therefore, the victims were able to be much more active in debating why it happened and what effect it had. Feminists argue that unless you consider the patriarchal nature of our society, you cannot explain why sex abuse is mostly males abusing females, nor can you explain why it only came to public attention as a serious problem once there was a strong feminist movement to speak up for the female victims.

Identifying sexual abuse

The three main categories of evidence are physical signs, behavioural/psychological signs, and disclosure by the victim.

Physical signs

Sometimes there are physical signs such as pregnancy, infection, genital bleeding or injury to the genital area that prove or strongly suggest that some sexual activity has occurred but, more often, any physical signs are ambiguous. In the 1980s, some paediatricians thought they had found a reliable indicator of sexual abuse in the anal dilatation test but this is now generally seen as indicative but not conclusive (Department of Health, 1988). Even when there is strong physical evidence, investigators may then face insuperable difficulties in establishing who the perpetrator was.

Behavioural/psychological signs

These tend to be indeterminate. Many victims show no behavioural or psychological signs at the time of the abuse (Monteleone and Brodeur, 1998: p. 143). But there are a number of signs which reveal the possibility of abuse, the most powerful being age-inappropriate knowledge of sex. However, most changes in a child's behaviour or mental state are non-specific to child sexual abuse and may be seen in a child under any-form of stress: anxiety, nightmares, hostility/anger, depression, running away from home, attempting suicide, drug addiction, involvement in prostitution and juvenile delinquency. If a child develops problematic behaviour, sexual abuse might be the cause, but independent evidence is needed to support it.

Disclosure by the victim

The main source of information is disclosure by the victim. However, for a variety of reasons, many victims feel unable to talk about the abuse while it is happening and while, as children, they are still vulnerable. They may disclose many years later as adults but they are usually then dealt with by the criminal justice system, not a child protection agency. When children begin to disclose, the process is often difficult and protracted and skill is needed in interviewing them (Aldridge and Wood, 1998; Milne and Bull, 1999).

The Home Office guidance *Achieving Best Evidence in Criminal Proceedings* (2001) is highly relevant when interviewing child victims. Videoed interviews are conducted – usually only by social workers or police officers who have undergone the relevant training – with the two aims of minimising trauma for the child by removing the need for the evidence to be repeated, and of obtaining evidence that meets the rules of evidence and so can be used in a criminal prosecution.

Characteristics of victims

Gender: girls outnumber boys as victims of sexual abuse; different studies estimate that they are between two and three times more vulnerable (Finkelhor, 1993). However, this finding may under-estimate the number of male victims since it may reflect male reluctance to report abuse (Finkelhor, 1981). The rate of male victims is higher in self-report surveys than in studies of officially known cases.

Age: cases are found in all age groups but the most vulnerable period for reported cases is from age 7 to 12 years (Finkelhor, 1993). It is probable, however, that abuse of younger children goes undetected because they are unable to tell anyone (Hewitt, 1998).

Social factors: having a mother who works outside the home, or who is ill or disabled, are associated with a higher risk. Other risk factors are parents with a conflicted relationship, or with alcohol or substance misuse problems (Brown et al., 1998). It has been suggested that the link between these risk factors and sexual abuse is that, in various ways, they expose children to risk as a result of limited parental care, supervision and protection (Fergusson and Mullen, 1999). Low family income and social status are *not* associated with any increased risk of sexual abuse (ibid.).

Disability: the incidence of sexual abuse of children with disabilities has been estimated to be 1.75 times the average rate (US DHHS, 1993).

Personal factors: there is some evidence that children who are physically attractive, small, and innocent and trusting are more likely to be targeted by perpetrators, as are children who appear vulnerable in some way, such as being passive, young, unhappy in appearance, or needy. Fergusson and Mullen (1999) conclude that children from families that show evidence of pervasive signs of dysfunction and difficulty are at higher than average risk of being victims of sexual abuse.

Perhaps all that can be concluded with any confidence from the research is that child sexual abuse is widespread, and that no particular sub-group in society is immune to it.

Characteristics of perpetrators

Age: very varied. The number of juvenile perpetrators may be under-estimated (Barbaree, Marshall and Hudson, 1993) and studies suggest that most sexual offenders develop deviant sexual interests prior to age 18 (Abel and Rouleau, 1990).

Gender: most are male – three-quarters or more in some studies (US DHHS, 1998). There is evidence that a significant minority of the male population has committed a sexual offence against a child. Finkelhor and Lewis (1988), in an American nationwide, random sample survey, found that between 4 per cent and 17 per cent of men admitted to molesting a child. Briere and Runtz (1989) found that 21 per cent of male undergraduates reported having experienced sexual attraction to children, and 7 per cent indicated they might consider having sex with a child if they knew they could avoid detection and punishment. It would be interesting to repeat these studies now and see if the same findings are obtained or whether the increased social awareness and condemnation of child sexual abuse is altering men's perceptions.

Women perpetrators may be under-estimated for cultural reasons – some of their abusive behaviour may be labelled inappropriate affection rather than abuse. They appear more likely to target boys than girls (Fergusson and Mullen, 1999).

Perpetrators' experience of child sexual abuse: studies indicate that 20–30 per cent of perpetrators were themselves victims of child sexual abuse; however, the majority of perpetrators were not themselves abused as children (Fergusson and Mullen, 1999).

Relationship to victim: the evidence suggests that the perpetrator is someone familiar to the child in the majority of cases, with boys more vulnerable to abuse by a stranger. In a large-scale community survey of adults reporting child abuse (Finkelhor et al., 1990), the findings were, for female and male respectively:

Family member 29 per cent and 11 per cent
Friend or acquaintance 41 per cent and 44 per cent
Stranger 21 per cent and 40 per cent

Grooming: how abuse can occur

A very powerful image of sexual abuse is that of a child being abducted by a stranger, raped or sexually assaulted, and then killed. Indeed, such tragic events do occur but they are relatively rare. In the majority of cases, abuse occurs within a relationship that has been slowly built up with the victim (Berliner and Conte, 1990). Once a victim is identified, the perpetrator may desensitise the child to sexual activity through a grooming process that involves a progression from non-sexual to sexual touch in the context of a gradually developing relationship. This typically starts with an apparently accidental touch and slowly progresses to more active abuse. Until recently, sex abuse was generally considered non-violent, with most experts estimating that violence accompanied it in only 20 per cent of cases, but now the use of violence and threats of violence are recognised as much more common, with a range of coercive tactics being used: separating the child from other protective adults, conditioning children through rewards and punishment, forcing children to observe violence against their mother, or using physical force or threatening gestures. The abuse is maintained by convincing the child it must be kept secret. Studies of victims show they do not disclose their abuse immediately, and sometimes not for many years, if at all.

Both perpetrators and victims have supported this account. Children also say the perpetrators try to justify the sexual contact by saying it is not really sexual, or just looking, or teaching them about sex, that is, they deny the harmful impact of what they are doing.

Internet abuse

The internet and other developments in ICT such as mobile phones have provided new mechanisms for abusing children. The main sources of danger are:

- the production and use of child pornography;
- online solicitation or 'grooming';
- exposure to materials that can cause psychological harm;
- harassment, intimidation, and bullying. (ECPAT International, 2005)

The Home Office has produced guidance on how to help children use the Internet safely (Home Office, 2005).

Ritual and organised abuse

Sexual abuse can be carried out by a number of abusers acting in an organised way. In the network, adults plan and develop social contacts with children for the purpose of gaining access to them to abuse them. Sometimes, the network may have an institutional base, such as being centred on a residential home. Sometimes, it is centred on an extended family network where there may be a history of abuse going back for generations. Special guidance has been provided for dealing with such complex cases (Home Office and Department of Health, 2002).

In ritual abuse, it is claimed that children are abused as part of a rite, such as worshipping the devil. Allegations of the existence of ritual abuse have been made for decades but, to date, there is no confirmed incident in the UK (La Fontaine, 1998).

Alleged cases of ritual abuse have produced some of the worst miscarriages of justice in the UK, as in Rochdale, Nottingham and Orkney. If the investigation is approached with an absolute conviction that ritual abuse has occurred, it seems some professionals are able to interpret seemingly innocent evidence to support the belief.

Long-term impact

Sexual abuse that involves penetration can result in acute, immediate injuries such as genital damage, pregnancy and sexually transmitted diseases. There are also serious psychological repercussions. Survivors often feel shame and guilt (Browne and Finkelhor, 1986). They have also been found to be less trusting and have a tendency to see a sexual or exploitative motivation in other's behaviour (Corby, 2000). Corby also reports that survivors can exhibit unusual and inappropriate sexual behaviour, such as increased sexual curiosity and frequent exposure of genitals, and simulated sex acts with siblings and friends (Mian, Marton and LeBaron, 1996).

Childhood sexual abuse has also been linked to difficulties in adult relationships and intimacy, with low rates of marriage, increased rates of relationship breakdown, multiple sexual partners, greater risk of sexually transmitted diseases, and increased rates of sexual revictimisation in adulthood (Mullen and Fleming, 1998).

Running theme: anti-discriminatory practice

There is considerable variation in the way that families express their affection in physical ways, in the amount of privacy between family members and in the openness with which sexuality is mentioned. It is important to assess the family context when judging the meaning of behaviour.

Running theme: the voice of the child

Professionals need to judge the evolving capacities of the child. Article 12 of the Convention on the Rights of the Child states that all children capable of expressing a view have the right to express that view freely and to have it taken seriously in accordance with their age and maturity. The 'evolving capacities of the child' captures the reality that children's ability to understand issues and form a view on them is not an either/or situation but one of a slowly developing competence. Practitioners therefore need to be able to gauge the child's level of development and help them participate in planning their care. Research paints a different picture, showing how hard it is to put principles into practice. Shemmings' (2000) research found that professionals tended to dichotomise children into those who were competent to participate and those who were not, with little sensitivity to the evolving capacities of the individual child.

Taking it *FURTHER*

Some victims have reported that they later regret disclosing the abuse because they found the response of the child protection system so distressing and disruptive. Some professionals have argued that children may need the guarantee of confidentiality in order to disclose (see Parton and Wattam, 1999: chapters 2 and 4). How can this be reconciled with the standard practice guidance in *Working Together to Safeguard Children* for professionals to share information when they have reason to believe that a child is suffering or is at risk of suffering significant harm? Why is confidentiality so important in helping relationships? If the professional remains silent, is there a danger of placing too much responsibility on the victim for addressing the problem? How might the system respond with more sensitivity by, for example, allowing a period for reflection, negotiation or dialogue so that professionals take account of how the child wants the situation dealt with, instead of rushing in with a standard response.

Further Reading

ECPAT INTERNATIONAL (2005) *Violence against Children in Cyberspace, Bangkok: ECPAT International. A comprehensive review of the dangers to which children are exposed in cyberspace and a summary of relevant research.*

D. FERGUSON AND P. MULLEN (1999) *Childhood Sexual Abuse: an evidence based perspective, Thousand Oaks, CA: Sage Publications. Provides a detailed summary and discussion of the research evidence.*

T. FURNIS (1991) *The Multi-Professional Handbook of Child Sexual Abuse, London: Routledge.*

HOME OFFICE (2005) *Good Practice Guidance for Search Service Providers and Advice to the Public on How to Search Safely, London: Home Office. A useful guide to help children use the Internet safely; Appendix A lists websites containing general child safety guidance relevant to Internet use.*

D. JONES AND P. RANCHANDANI (1999) *Child Sexual Abuse, Oxford: Radcliffe. A review of the research evidence.*

J. LA FONTAINE (1990) *Child Sexual Abuse, Cambridge: Polity Press. A study of child sexual abuse from a sociological perspective.*

N. PARTON AND C. WATTAM (EDS) (1999) *Child Sexual Abuse:* responding to the *experiences of children, Chichester: Wiley. Sets out a child-centred approach to dealing with child sexual abuse, gives a good overview of the problems experienced by children in reporting abuse, and has many helpful chapters on specific practice issues.*

2.12

what can be done to make children safer?

Learning outcomes

This section will help you to understand:

- The different levels at which prevention strategies can be implemented.

- The range of universal and targeted services that contribute to reducing abuse and neglect.

- The evidence on key intervention strategies for preventing the recurrence of abuse and neglect.

- The evidence on the effectiveness of therapies for helping victims.

Levels of prevention

There are four significantly different stages at which preventive strategies may be implemented.

Level 1: Preventing abuse and neglect from occurring.
Level 2: Preventing low-level problems, including abuse and neglect, from getting worse.

Level 3: Preventing child abuse and neglect from recurring.
Level 4: Preventing abuse and neglect from causing long-term harm.

In the *Every Child Matters* policy of shifting from a reactive to a preventive approach, the aim is to strengthen levels 1 and 2 so that fewer children reach levels 3 and 4. However, since this book is on child protection, this chapter will concentrate on levels 3 and 4, the families known to the child protection system, with only a brief look at the primary and secondary levels of prevention.

The Evidence Based Practice movement has led to a greater interest in reporting research and identifying its practice implications (Chaffin and Friedrich, 2004), with the many websites, listed on p. 57 offering a growing list of research summaries. Evaluative studies, however, are still relatively scarce and many show only modest success at best. They do offer some valuable guidance, though, as well as emphasising the need for rigorous evaluation and for continuing to look for therapeutic ideas. The subject is too big to permit a comprehensive review so the focus in this section will be on the interventions most commonly used in the UK. For other interventions or more up-to-date findings, readers should consult the research websites.

Level 1   Preventing abuse and neglect from occurring

Preventing children from being harmed at all by abuse or neglect is clearly preferable to stopping it happening again. Primary prevention strategies are typically aimed at children's well-being in general. Abuse and neglect are only two of the many factors that can have an adverse impact on children's health and development and many of the factors that make abuse and neglect more likely, such as economic and social stresses, or poor health in the parents, can also have a directly harmful effect on children. Therefore, strategies to reduce these factors will have a knock-on effect on reducing abuse and neglect.

Primary prevention strategies can be universal or targeted. In the UK, there are a number of universal services – health, education, housing, income support – that are designed to help all members of society meet their needs. The adequacy of these services affects the degree of primary prevention achieved. Changes in the Social Security system in the 1980s, for example, contributed to the steep increase in children living in poverty (rising from 10 per cent in 1979 to 33 per cent in 1997) and this will have had an adverse impact on many children. The current government aim is to ensure that no child is brought up in poverty and, if successful, this should be a valuable preventive strategy.

Many of the current preventive strategies are targeted at groups or neighbourhoods considered to be at higher than average risk of poor outcomes. Risk-assessment instruments, such as Onset and Ryogens, are being used to identify children considered at risk of juvenile offending or anti-social behaviour so that services can be targeted on them.

In relation to abuse and neglect, SureStart is the most relevant service. This began in the neighbourhoods identified as having high levels of deprivation and aims to enhance service provision for all families in the area, thereby improving children's development. To date, the evaluations of SureStart have produced disappointing results, with some small signs of improvement but also some indications that sub-groups, such as children of teenage mothers, are faring worse in SureStart areas (SureStart, 2005). It has been argued that the schemes need more time to demonstrate their effectiveness.

Level 2   *Preventing low-level problems from getting worse*

In the *Every Child Matters* agenda, children with low-level problems are classed as having 'additional needs'; they are considered at higher than average risk of developing more serious problems if help is not provided. By introducing the Common Assessment Framework and encouraging a multi-disciplinary approach, the government aims to improve early assessment and response to need. The strategies for helping these children are diverse, with all services expected to play some part in provision. It is too early to evaluate the overall impact of this policy change or even to identify what types of intervention are being commonly used.

Level 3   *Preventing child abuse and neglect from recurring*

The evidence indicates limited success in preventing further abuse or neglect. Farmer and Owen's (1995) study found that 25 per cent of children placed on the child protection register had been re-abused by the time of the follow-up interview at 20 months. Ellaway et al. (2004) followed up, for three years, a cohort of 69 babies under 1 year old after a child protection investigation had concluded that physical abuse had taken place. Forty-nine of the babies were returned home and, of these, 15 were further abused, a rate of 31 per cent. The re-abuse was not just physical but included neglect. Moreover, not only were they at risk, but so too were their siblings. Of the total cohort, there were child protection concerns about siblings in 49 per cent of the cases.

Using assessments to plan interventions

Families who abuse or neglect their children are a highly diverse group and it is unlikely that any one intervention will be useful in all cases. Help needs to be tailored to the assessed needs of the family, and the better the assessment the more it will generate specific ideas about how to improve the children's safety and well-being. Going beyond the surface presentation of problems and trying to understand their deeper causes will lead to more precise intervention plans. Policy emphasises the importance of assessing not just the child's safety but also their wider developmental needs and the parenting capacity in the family and environment. The Assessment Framework and the various forms in the Integrated Children's System are designed to encourage such a holistic and thorough assessment. A thorough understanding of the family's history is crucial in identifying patterns of behaviour and dominant points of stress where daily hassles may escalate into more serious abuse. Multi-disciplinary assessment is likely to be more sensitive to the range of problems in a family, offering a more expert overall assessment than any one professional could provide.

Running theme: the voice of the child

Research on the use of the Assessment Framework shows that social work practice continues to exclude children from fully participating in decisions that are likely to affect them (Cleaver, Walker with Meadows, 2004: 248). When asked how things could be improved, children in this study reiterated the issues found in earlier research. They wanted professionals to:

- take time to explain to them what is happening and why
- listen to and respect their views and experiences
- believe what they said
- talk to the people they think are important
- provide them with something to remind them of what was decided.

Home visitation programmes

In the UK, health visitors have long had a preventive role in offering advice and support to families. Although a universal service, they tend to target families that appear vulnerable. There is good evidence of their effectiveness in primary prevention of abuse and neglect (MacMillan et al., 1994) but they appear to be less effective in preventing recurrence. MacMillan et al. (2005) conducted a random controlled trial on 163 families with a history of one child being exposed to physical abuse or neglect, in which the experimental group received home visitation in addition to the standard response. A higher rate of abuse was recorded in the experimental group. This disappointing result may be due to the 'surveillance effect' – their greater visibility to professionals leading to more incidents of abuse being noted.

Parenting classes

These can be used at all levels of prevention, including after abuse or neglect have occurred. Macdonald (2001: 152) summarises their range of aims:

- Providing information about child development, health, hygiene, safety, etc.
- Helping parents reconsider and reframe 'age-inappropriate' expectations and misattributions.
- Enhancing the quality of child–parent relationships by, for example, teaching play skills, structuring the day so that they set aside some time for themselves and their child(ren).
- Developing parents' ability to monitor and track their children's behaviour and respond appropriately, including the management of challenging behaviour.
- Increasing support networks.

Remember the importance of linking your assessment and your plan. If you decide to offer parenting classes to parents, you should be able to identify which of the above aims you are hoping to achieve and why.

Besides having diverse aims, programmes use a range of methods, so it is not possible to reach a single judgement about parenting classes. Barlow (1997) reviewed the available evidence and concluded:

- Group-based programmes generally produced better results than individual programmes.
- Behavioural programmes produced better results than relationship-based (Adlerian) or PET (Parent Effectiveness Training) Programmes.
- One study showed that a behavioural programme produced significant changes in child behaviour irrespective of the method used – such as group or individual, phone or home visits.

A later review, looking specifically at parenting classes for teenage parents, reached a cautious but slightly optimistic conclusion:

The findings of the review are based on a small number of studies, and are therefore limited. The results suggest, however, that parenting programmes may be effective in improving a range of psychosocial and developmental outcomes for teenage mothers and their children. Further research is needed, particularly that which includes long-term follow-up of the children of teen parents and the role of young fathers as well as young mothers. (Coren and Barlow, 2002)

Summarising evidence on who is *not* likely to receive sufficient help from parenting classes, Macdonald (2001: 155) lists the following factors, all of which are frequently found in the families known to the child protection system:

- Poor parental adjustment, particularly maternal depression
- Maternal stress and low socio-economic status
- Social isolation of mother
- Relationship problems
- Extrafamilial conflict
- The problems are severe and/or long-standing
- Parental misperception of the deviance of their children's behaviour.

Parent–child interaction therapy

A behavioural programme for physically abusive parents has shown evidence of success with a significantly reduced rate of future physical abuse (Chaffin et al., 2004; Chambless and Ollendick, 2001).

Family therapy

There are two main forms: (a) behavioural family therapy, based on social learning theory, which uses structured, behavioural exchange programmes to increase positive behaviours and communication and problem-solving; (b) family systems therapy, covering a range of different methods but with a common assumption that the family is a rule-governed system, not just a group of individuals (Hazelrigg, Cooper and Bourduin, 1987). Given the diversity in specific forms of therapy and the scarcity of studies, it is hard to reach any general evaluation, but the behavioural approaches have more support than the systems ones (Macdonald, 2001: 177).

Family group conferences

These originated in New Zealand and are becoming increasingly common in the UK (see Family Rights Group, 2002, for a brief guide). The core idea is that the family is brought together to find the best plan for tackling their problems and providing good care for the children. At the conference, the decision makers are the family members, not the professionals. They appeal to many because of the way that they empower the family. However, there are few evaluative studies available. One three-year trial in Sweden found that children dealt with through family group conferences had higher rates of re-referral for abuse than those who received the standard approach but tended to get less intrusive support from the child protection services (Sundell and Vinnerljung, 2004).

Multisystemic therapy

These programmes offering intensive support to families where abuse or neglect have occurred have become popular in the USA. However, the evidence on effectiveness is, as yet, lacking. Littell, Popa and Forsythe (2005: 4) reviewed the available studies and concluded:

> Results of eight randomised controlled trials of Multisystemic Therapy (MST) conducted in the USA, Canada, and Norway indicate that it is premature to draw conclusions about the effectiveness of MST compared with other services. Results are inconsistent across studies that vary in quality and context. There is no information about the effects of MST compared with no treatment. There is no evidence that MST has harmful effects.

Parents' problems

One strategy for improving children's care and safety is to ensure that the parents receive help for major problems. The Department of Health stresses this point in its guidance on the Assessment Framework (2000: para. 4.5):

> In most situations, meeting children's needs will almost always involve responding also to the needs of family members. The two are closely connected and it is rarely possible to promote the welfare of children without promoting the welfare of significant adults in their lives.

The three that are most commonly found in child protection work, and are known to have an adverse impact on parenting (Cleaver, Unell and Aldgate, 1999) are alcohol and substance misuse, domestic violence, and mental illness.

Alcohol and substance misuse SCIE (2006) provide a research briefing that summarises how parenting capacity can be affected by parental substance misuse and how this might be managed. It notes that professionals often fail to evaluate the impact of substance misuse on parenting capacity, which may adversely affect their ability to attend to the emotional, physical and developmental needs of their children, both in the short and long term. It contains many useful references to policies and practice issues.

Tunnard (2002) also reviews research and policy and provides an excellent account of how different drugs impact on parenting behaviour. She also draws attention to the imbalance in government and professional attention to drugs and alcohol misuse. Alcohol misuse is far more common but the misuse of drugs arouses more concern and action.

Domestic violence   Domestic violence is of concern for two reasons: (i) it often co-exists with child abuse, and (ii) its occurrence has a harmful impact on the children in the family (Humphreys and Mullender, 2005). Society's concern about it has risen markedly in recent years, with more effort being put into offering help to victims. See, for example, the Metropolitan Police Domestic Violence Strategy (2001).

Ramsey, Rivas and Feder (2005) provide a review of strategies for dealing with domestic violence. Examining 36 studies – on advocacy, support groups, counselling and therapy, and system-centred interventions – they concluded that advocacy worked best for women still living in the abusive relationship, system-centred approaches increased referral rates at least in the short term, and there is some evidence that counselling is useful, after the woman has left the abusive relationship, for treatment of depression and low self-esteem.

Mental illness   Tunnard (2003: 40) offers a wide-ranging review of the problems presented by parental mental ill-health and the practice guidance offered by research. Her key findings are:

- Family members – parents as well as children – need to have their fears allayed, and to have access to information, specialist services, support that is consistent and continuous, and the same life chances and opportunities as other parents and children.
- Obstacles to achieving good outcomes for children and parents include a fragmented response by adult and children's services, a lack of attention to the needs of individuals, and an undue focus on negatives rather than strengths.
- Parents, children and professionals have many ideas in common about what might make a positive difference to the quality of life of families living with mental health problems.
- A sympathetic response from professionals, early attention to difficulties, support for different family members, a specific focus on particular problems, and using families' own experiences to identify needs and possible solutions are common proposals for improving practice.

Level 4 *Preventing abuse and neglect from causing long-term harm*

Given the evidence on the long-term harm caused by abuse and neglect, interventions to minimise that impact are to be welcomed. However, it is an area of work that, in practice, tends to get little attention in its own right, with most professional effort going into improving children's current safety and level of care until such time as the harm shows up in problematic behaviour. A number of therapeutic approaches are available but there are few evaluative studies of them.

OVC (2004) provides the largest review to date of mental health interventions for children who were victims of abuse. Funded by the US Office for Victims of Crime, it covers 24 interventions for children, parents, the parent–child relationship, and offenders. It classifies them on theoretical basis, clinical/anecdotal literature, acceptance/use in practice, potential for harm, and degree of empirical support. The latter is rated on a six-point scale:

1 = well-supported, efficacious treatment
2 = supported and probably efficacious treatment
3 = supported and acceptable treatment
4 = promising and acceptable treatment
5 = innovative or novel treatment
6 = concerning treatment.

Only one method – trauma-focused cognitive-behavioural therapy merited a rating of well-supported and efficacious (Cohen and Mannarino, 1997). One treatment – attachment therapy – was rated as concerning with a significant potential for harm. Full details are available from www.musc.edu/cvc/.

Returning children home

Once children have been removed from their birth parents because of abuse or neglect, professionals are faced with the decision of whether and when they can safely return home. Biehal (2006: 1) provides a valuable summary of the relevant research findings in the UK and the USA, including:

- Many children return home quite quickly but the probability of return declines sharply after six months. Time in care appears to be related to a variety of other factors which make return less probable.
- Children placed because of physical or sexual abuse are more likely to return home than those placed due to neglect.

- Evidence from a small number of UK studies suggests that between one-third and one-half of children who return home may subsequently re-enter care.
- There has been little research on the outcomes of reunion, but the evidence suggests that some children who return experience re-abuse or neglect.
- The limited evidence on psychosocial outcomes of reunion suggests that reunited children may have more serious emotional and behavioural problems than those who remain looked after in care.

Research on effective working relationships

Regardless of the intervention chosen, there is evidence that effective interpersonal skills can increase the likelihood of establishing rapport with service users, gaining their co-operation, and avoiding drop-out (e.g., Patterson and Forgatch, 1985). 'Helpers who are cold, closed down, and judgemental are not as likely to involve clients as collaborators as are those who are warm, supportive, and empathic' (Gambrill, 2006: 409). Skills identified as contributing to relationship-building and positive outcomes include:

> therapist credibility
> empathic understanding and affirmation of the service user
> skill in engaging the user
> a focus on the user's concerns
> skill in directing the user's attention to the user's emotional experiences.

Dale's (2004) qualitative study of 18 families provides some vivid illustration of parents' good and bad experiences of working relationships. The positive findings echoed those listed above: for example, one parent valued 'eye-to-eye contact – being able to talk to each other – say anything we want to each other'. Negative comments reflected the opposite qualities of helpers – of being 'uninterested, ineffective, unsupportive, unreliable and unavailable' (2004: 153).

 Taking it **FURTHER**

In social work, there is a long history of hostility or indifference to cognitive-behavioural methods of working yet these have produced the strongest evidence of effectiveness with a range of problems found in child protection work (Macdonald, 2001). This raises the question of how much freedom professionals should have in choosing interventions. Is it defensible for them to disregard apparently effective interventions that, for some reason, they themselves do not wish to use? The cognitive-behavioural approach has been criticised for dealing only with surface issues and not getting to the deeper causes of problem behaviour. Others argue that if the surface issues that it solves are physical assaults on children, this is an outcome worth achieving.

Further reading

The websites listed on p. 57 are the best resource for obtaining the most up-to-date information on evaluative studies.

G. MACDONALD (2001) *Effective Interventions for Child Abuse and Neglect,* Chichester: Wiley. *Provides a well-researched and wide-ranging review of evaluative research, with good discussion of the issues in conducting rigorous studies.*

NATIONAL CHILDREN'S BUREAU (2004) *'Group-based parenting programmes and reducing children's behaviour problems', Highlight No. 211 available to members from www.ncb.org.uk. A brief summary of the evidence on parenting programmes.*

On the impact of parental problems on childcare:

H. CLEAVER, I. UNELL AND J. ALDGATE (1999) *Children's Needs – Parenting Capacity: the impact of parental mental illness, problem alcohol and drug use, and domestic violence on children's development, London: HMSO.*

SOCIAL CARE INSTITUTE FOR EXCELLENCE (2006) *'Research Briefing 6: parenting capacity and substance misuse', London, SCIE. Available from www. scie.org.uk.*

part three*

study, writing and revision skills

*in collaboration with David McIlroy

3.1	
general introduction	

The thinking and writing skills needed to complete a child protection course successfully are of equal value in your later professional work. Writing a well-researched and coherently argued essay has much in common with preparing a well-evidenced court report which clearly shows the reasoning that leads to your conclusions and recommendations. Moreover, you will – or, at least, should – go on learning throughout your professional career. Families and their problems are infinitely varied and complex so there is always scope for acquiring new insights.

If you work your way carefully through this part you should at the end be better equipped to profit from your lectures, benefit from your seminars, construct your essays efficiently, develop effective revision strategies and respond comprehensively to the pressures of exam situations. All of these skills will be useful in professional practice.

In the five sections that lie ahead you will be presented with:

• checklists and bullet points to focus your attention on key issues;
• exercises to help you participate actively in the learning experience;
• illustrations and analogies to enable you to anchor learning principles in everyday events and experiences;
• worked examples to demonstrate the use of such features as structure, headings and continuity;
• tips that provide practical advice for your study of child protection.

Each student should decide how much effort they would like to invest in each exercise presented, according to individual preferences and requirements. Some of the points in the exercises will be covered in the text either before or after the exercise. You might prefer to read each section right through before going back to tackle the exercises. Suggested answers are provided in italics after some of the exercises, so avoid these if you prefer to work through the exercises on your own. The aim is to prompt you to reflect on the material, remember what you have read and trigger you to add your own thoughts.

Finally, the overall aim of the section is to point out to you the keys for academic and personal development. The twin emphases of academic development and personal qualities are stressed throughout. By giving attention to these factors you will give yourself the toolkit you will need to excel in your studies and your work with families.

| 3.2 | |
| how to get the most out of your lectures | |

What this section will give you: how to –

- make the most of your lecture notes
- prepare your mind for new terms
- develop an independent approach to learning
- write efficient summary notes from lectures
- take the initiative in building on your lectures.

Keeping in context

According to higher educational commentators and advisors, best-quality learning is facilitated when it is set within an overall learning context. It should be the responsibility of your tutors to provide a context for you to learn in, but it is your responsibility to see this overall context, and you can do this even before your first lecture begins. Such a panoramic view can be achieved by becoming familiar with the outline content of both a given subject and the entire study programme. Before you go into each lecture you should briefly remind yourself of where it fits into the overall scheme of things. Think, for example, of how more confident you feel when you move into a new city (for example to attend university) once you become familiar with your bearings – that is, where you live in relation to college, shops, stores, buses, trains, places of entertainment, etc.

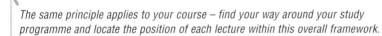

The same principle applies to your course – find your way around your study programme and locate the position of each lecture within this overall framework.

Use of lecture notes

It is always beneficial to do some preliminary reading before you enter a lecture. If lecture notes are provided in advance (e.g. electronically), then print these out, read over them and bring them with you to the lecture. You can insert question marks on issues where you will need further clarification. Some lecturers prefer to provide full notes, some prefer to make skeleton outlines available and some prefer to issue no notes at all! If notes are provided, take full advantage and supplement these with your own notes as you listen. In a later section on memory techniques you will see that humans possess ability for 're-learning savings' – i.e. it is easier to learn material the second time round, as it is evident that we have a capacity to hold residual memory deposits. So some basic preparation will equip you with a great advantage – you will be able to 'tune in' and think more clearly about the lecture than you would have done without the preliminary work.

If you set yourself too many tedious tasks at the early stages of your academic programme you may lose some motivation and momentum. A series of short, simple, achievable tasks can give your mind the 'lubrication' you need. For example, you are more likely to maintain preliminary reading for a lecture if you set modest targets.

Mastering technical terms

Let us assume that in an early lecture you are introduced to a series of new terms such as 'anti-discriminatory practice', 'ecological' and 'genogram'. New words can be threatening, especially if you have to face a string of them in one lecture. The uncertainty about the new terms may impair your ability to benefit fully from the lecture and therefore hinder the quality of your learning. Some subjects require technical terms and the use of them is unavoidable. However, when you have heard a term a number of times it will not seem as daunting as it initially was. It is claimed that individuals may have particular strengths in the scope of their vocabulary. Some people may have a good recognition vocabulary – they immediately know what a word means when they read it or hear it in context. Others have a good command of language when they speak – they have an ability to recall words freely. Still others are more fluent in recall when they write – words seem to flow rapidly for them when they engage in the dynamics of writing. You can work at developing all three approaches in your course, and the checklist below may be of some help in mastering and marshalling the terms you hear in lectures.

In terms of learning new words, it will be very useful if you can first try to work out what they mean from their context when you first encounter them. You might be much better at this than you imagine, especially if there is only one word in the sentence that you do not understand.

Checklist: Mastering terms used in your lectures

✓ Read lecture notes before the lectures and list any unfamiliar terms.

✓ Read over the listed terms until you are familiar with their sound.

✓ Try to work out meanings of terms from their context.

✓ Do not suspend learning the meaning of a term indefinitely.

✓ Write out a sentence that includes the new word (do this for each word).

✓ Meet with other students and test each other with the technical terms.

✓ Jot down new words you hear in lectures and check out the meaning soon afterwards.

Your confidence will greatly increase when you begin to follow the flow of arguments that contain technical terms, and more especially when you can freely use the terms yourself in speaking and writing.

Developing independent study

In the current educational ethos there are the twin aims of cultivating teamwork/group activities and independent learning. There is not necessarily a conflict between the two, as they should complement each other. For example, if you are committed to independent learning you have more to offer other students when you work in small groups, and you will also be prompted to follow up on the leads given by them. Furthermore, the guidelines given to you in lectures are designed to lead you into deeper independent study. The issues raised in lectures are pointers to provide direction and structure for your extended personal pursuit. Your aim should invariably be to build on what you are given, and you should never think of merely returning the bare bones of the lecture material in a coursework essay or exam.

It is always very refreshing to a marker to be given work from a student that contains recent studies that the examiner had not previously encountered.

Note-taking strategy

Note-taking in lectures is an art that you will only perfect with practice and by trial and error. Each student should find the formula that works best for him or her. What works for one, may not work for the other. Some students can write more quickly than others, some are better at shortcuts than others and some are better at deciphering their own scrawl! The problem will always be to try to find a balance between concentrating beneficially on what you hear, and making sufficient notes that will enable you to comprehend later what you have heard. You should not however become frustrated by the fact that you will not immediately understand or remember everything you have heard.

Guidelines for note-taking in lectures

- Develop the note-taking strategy that works best for you.
- Work at finding a balance between listening and writing.
- Make some use of optimal shortcuts (e.g. a few key words may summarise a story).
- Too much writing may impair the flow of the lecture for you.
- Too much writing may impair the quality of your notes.
- Some limited notes are better than none.
- Good note-taking may facilitate deeper processing of information.
- It is essential to 'tidy up' notes as soon as possible after a lecture.
- Reading over notes soon after lectures will consolidate your learning.

Developing the lecture

Some educationalists have criticised the value of lectures because they allege that these are a mode of merely 'passive learning'. This can certainly be an accurate conclusion to arrive at (that is, if students approach lectures in the wrong way) and lecturers can work to devise ways of making a lecture more interactive. For example, they can make use of handouts that include questions or by posing questions during the lecture and giving time out for students to reflect on these. Other possibilities are short discussions at given junctures in the lecture or use of small groups within the session. As a student you do not have to enter a lecture in passive mode, and you can ensure that you are not merely a passive recipient of information by taking steps to develop the lecture yourself. A list of suggestions is presented below to help you take the initiative in developing the lecture content.

Checklist to ensure that the lecture is not merely a passive experience

✓ Try to interact with the lecture material by asking questions.

✓ Highlight points that you would like to develop in personal study.

✓ Trace connections between the lecture and other parts of your study programme.

✓ Bring together notes from the lecture and other sources.

✓ Restructure the lecture outline into your own preferred format.

✓ Think of ways in which aspects of the lecture material can be applied.

✓ Design ways in which aspects of the lecture material can be illustrated.

✓ If the lecturer invites questions, make a note of all the questions asked.

✓ Follow up on issues of interest that have arisen out of the lecture.

3.3	
how to make the most of seminars	

What this section will give you: how to –

- be aware of the value of seminars
- focus on links to learning
- recognise qualities you can use repeatedly
- manage potential problems in seminars
- prepare yourself adequately for seminars.

Not to be under-estimated

Seminars are often optional in a degree programme and sometimes poorly attended because they are under-estimated. Some students may be convinced that the lecture is the truly authoritative way to receive quality information. Undoubtedly, lectures play an important role in an academic programme, but seminars have a unique contribution to learning that will complement lectures.

On a social work course, seminars are often the place where students are helped to make links between theory and practice, to apply their learning to case material and think through how the two elements of the course can be integrated.

Checklist: Some useful features of seminars

✓   Can identify problems that you had not thought of.

✓   Can clear up confusing issues.

✓   Allows you to ask questions and make comments.

✓   Can link theory and practice.

✓   Can help you develop friendships and teamwork.

✓   Enables you to refresh and consolidate your knowledge.

✓   Can help you sharpen motivation and redirect study efforts.

An asset to complement other learning activities

In higher education at the present time there is emphasis on variety – variety in delivery, learning experience, learning styles and assessment methods. The seminar is deemed to hold an important place within the overall scheme of teaching, learning and assessment. In some programmes the seminars are directly linked to the assessment task. Whether or not they have such a place in your course, they will provide you with a unique opportunity to learn and develop.

In a seminar you will hear a variety of contributions, and different perspectives and emphases. You will have the chance to interrupt and the experience of being interrupted! You will also learn that you can get things wrong and still survive! It is often the case that when one student admits that they did not know some important piece of information, other students quickly follow with the same admission. If you can learn to ask questions and not feel stupid, then seminars will give you an asset for learning and a life-long educational skill. A seminar can provide a valuable model for case discussion in later practice, providing a safe place in which you can acknowledge your uncertainty and look critically at your work in a supportive atmosphere.

Creating the right climate in seminars

It has been said that we have been given only one mouth to talk, but two ears to listen. One potential problem with seminars is that some students may take a while to learn this lesson, and other students may have to help hasten them on the way (graciously but firmly!). In lectures your main role is to listen and take notes, but in seminars there is the challenge of striking the balance between listening and speaking. It is important to make a beginning in speaking, even if it is just to repeat something that you agree with. You can also learn to disagree in an agreeable way. For example, you can question what someone else has said but pose this in a good tone, for example, 'If that is the case, does that not mean that ... ?' In addition, it is perfectly possible to disagree with others by avoiding personal attacks such as: 'That was a really stupid thing to say', or 'I thought you knew better than that', or 'I'm surprised that you don't know that by now.' Educationalists say that it is important to have the right climate to learn in, and the avoidance of unnecessary conflict will foster such a climate.

Some strategies that teachers may use are: appoint someone to guide and control the discussion, invite individuals to prepare in advance to make a contribution, hand out agreed discussion questions at some point prior to the seminar, stress at the beginning that no one should monopolise the discussion, and emphasise that there must be no personal attacks on any individual (state clearly what this means). Also you could invite and encourage quieter students to participate and assure each person that their contribution is valued.

The skills needed to create the right climate in a seminar are also needed in a child protection conference if it is to achieve its purpose of enabling a sharing of information, an appraisal of a family's strengths and needs, and a plan for helping them.

Links in learning and transferable skills

An important principle in learning to progress from shallow to deep learning is developing the capacity to make connecting links between themes or topics and across subjects. This also applies to the various learning activities such as lectures, seminars, fieldwork, computer searches and private study. Another question to ask is: 'What skills can I develop, or improve on, from seminars, that I can use across my study programme?' A couple of examples of key skills are the ability to communicate and the capacity to work within a team. These are skills that you will be able to use at various points in your course (transferable), but you are not likely to develop them within the formal setting of a lecture.

A key question that you should bring to every seminar – 'How does this seminar connect with my other learning activities and my assessments?'

An opportunity to contribute

If you have never made a contribution to a seminar before, you may need something to use as an 'ice breaker'. It does not matter if your first contribution is only a sentence or two – the important thing is to make a start. One way to do this is to make brief notes as others contribute, and while doing this, a question or two might arise in your mind. If your first contribution is a question, that is a good start. Or it may be that you will be able to point out some connection between what others have said, or identify conflicting opinions that need to be resolved. If you have already begun making contributions, it is important that you keep the momentum going, and do not allow yourself to lapse back into the safe cocoon of shyness.

EXERCISE

See if you can suggest how you might resolve some of the following problems that might hinder you from making a contribution to seminars.

One student who dominates and monopolises the discussion.

Someone else has already said what you really want to say.

Fear that someone else will correct you and make you feel stupid.

Feel that your contribution might be seen as short and shallow.

A previous negative experience puts you off making any more contributions.

Strategies for benefiting from your seminar experience

If you are required to bring a presentation to your seminar, you might want to consult a full chapter on presentations in a complementary study guide (McIlroy, 2003). Alternatively, you may be content with the summary bullet points below.

Checklist: How to benefit from seminars

✓ Do some preparatory reading.

✓ Familiarise yourself with the main ideas to be addressed.

✓ Make notes during the seminar.

✓ Make some verbal contribution, even a question.

✓ Remind yourself of the skills you can develop.

✓ Trace learning links from the seminar to other subjects/topics on your programme.

✓ Make brief bullet points for what you should follow up on.

✓ Read over your notes as soon as possible after the seminar.

✓ Continue discussion with fellow students after the seminar has ended.

If required to give a presentation –

- Have a practice run with friends.
- If using visuals, do not obstruct them.
- Check out beforehand that all equipment works.
- Space out points clearly on visuals (large and legible).
- Time talk by visuals (e.g. five slides by 15-minute talk = 3 minutes per slide).
- Make sure your talk synchronises with the slide on view at any given point.
- Project your voice so that all in the room can hear.
- Inflect your voice and do not stand motionless.
- Spread eye contact around your audience.
- Avoid twin extremes of fixed gaze at individuals and never looking at anyone.
- Better to fall a little short of time allocation than run over it.
- Be selective in what you choose to present.
- Map out where you are going and summarise main points at the end.

3.4

essay-writing tips

What this section will give you: how to –

- quickly engage with the main arguments
- channel your passions constructively
- note your main arguments in an outline
- find and focus on your central topic questions
- weave quotations into your essay.

Getting into the flow

In essay writing one of your first aims should be to get your mind active and engaged with your subject. Tennis players like to go out onto the court and hit the ball back and forth just before the competitive match begins. This allows them to judge the bounce of the ball, feel its weight against their racket, get used to the height of the net, the parameters of the court and other factors such as temperature, light, sun and the crowd. In the same way you can 'warm up' for your essay by tossing the ideas to and fro within your head before you begin to write. This will allow you to think within the framework of your topic, and this will be especially important if you are coming to the subject for the first time.

The tributary principle

A tributary is a stream that runs into a main river as it wends its way to the sea. Similarly, in an essay you should ensure that every idea you introduce is moving toward the overall theme you are addressing. Your idea might of course be relevant to a sub-heading that is in turn relevant to a main heading. Every idea you introduce is to be a 'feeder' into the flowing theme. In addition to tributaries, there can also be 'distributaries', which are streams that flow away from the river. In an essay these would represent the ideas that run away from the main stream of thought and leave the reader trying to work out what their relevance might have been. It is one thing to have grasped your subject thoroughly, but quite another to convince your reader that this is the case. Your aim should be to build up ideas sentence by sentence and paragraph by paragraph, until you have communicated your clear purpose to the reader.

> *It is important in essay writing that you not only include material that is relevant, but that you also make the linking statements that show the connection to the reader.*

Listing and linking the key concepts

All subjects will have central concepts that can sometimes be usefully labelled by a single word. Course textbooks may include a glossary of terms and these provide a direct route to the beginning of efficient mastery of the topic. The central words or terms are the essential raw materials that you will need to build upon. Ensure that you learn the words and their definitions, and that you can go on to link the key words together so that in your learning activities you will add understanding to your basic memory work.

> *It is useful to list your key words under general headings if that is possible and logical. You may not always see the connections immediately, but when you later come back to a problem that seemed intractable you will often find that your thinking is much clearer.*

❝ Write an essay on 'The causes of child abuse' ❞

You might decide to draft your outline points in the following manner (or you may prefer to use a mind-map approach):

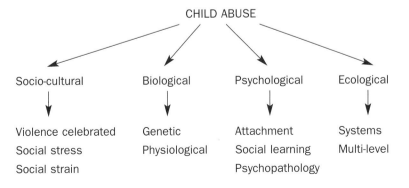

An adversarial system

In higher education students are required to make the transition from descriptive to critical writing. If you can, think of the critical approach as like a law case that is being conducted where there is both a prosecution and a defence. Your concern should be for objectivity, transparency and fairness. No matter how passionately you may feel about a given cause you must not allow information to be filtered out because of your personal prejudice. An essay is not to become a crusade for a cause in which the contrary arguments are not addressed in an even-handed manner. This means that you should show awareness that opposite views are held and you should at least represent these as accurately as possible.

All of these points apply with equal force in your professional practice. You must not allow your assessment of a family to become a crusade to convince others of your opinion. Injustice and mistakes arise when professionals act like barristers, presenting and defending one point of view only and failing to give due consideration and respect to the other side's version. You should see yourself more as a detective who is searching for the truth, and remain open to new information and new interpretations of the evidence you have.

Stirring up passions

The above points do not of course mean that you are not entitled to a personal persuasion or to feel passionately about your subject. On the contrary, such feelings may well be a marked advantage if you can bring them under control and channel them into balanced, effective writing (see example below). Some students may be struggling at the other end of the spectrum – being required to write on a topic about which they feel quite indifferent. As you engage with your topic and toss the ideas around in your mind, you may find that your interest is stimulated, if only at an intellectual level initially. How strongly you feel about a topic, or how much you are interested in it, may depend on whether you choose the topic yourself or whether it has been given to you as an obligatory assignment.

It is important that in a large project (such as a dissertation) you choose a topic for which you can maintain your motivation, momentum and enthusiasm.

Structuring an outline

Whenever you sense a flow of inspiration to write on a given subject, it is essential that you put this into a structure that will allow your inspiration to be communicated clearly. It is a basic principle in all walks of life that structure and order facilitate good communication. Therefore, when you have the flow of inspiration in your essay you must get this into a structure that will allow the marker to recognise the true quality of your work. For example you might plan for an introduction, followed by three main headings, each with several sub-headings (see example below), and rounded off with a conclusion. Moreover, you may decide not to include your headings in your final presentation – that is, just use them initially to structure and balance your arguments. Once you have drafted this outline you can then easily sketch an introduction, and you will have been well prepared for the conclusion when you arrive at that point.

"Write an essay that assesses whether the new *Every Child Matters* policy will achieve its goals."

1   The goals of the *Every Child Matters* policy

  (a)   to improve detection of serious child abuse and neglect (response to Climbie report)
  (b)   to counter inequalities, ensuring all children fulfil their potential
  (c)   to reduce major problems: youth offending, teenage pregnancy, poor educational achievement.

2   How are they to be achieved?

  (a)   improving identification and early assessment of need so problems do not get worse
  (b)   improving response through better inter-agency working
  (c)   improving provision.

3   Possible limitations

  (a)   limited knowledge about predicting which children will have problems
  (b)   limited effectiveness of preventive interventions
  (c)   chronic problems of inter-agency collaboration may continue
  (d)   inadequate resources to meet increased amount of assessed need.

Finding major questions

When you are constructing a draft outline for an essay or project, you should ask what is the major question or questions you wish to address. It would be useful to make a list of all the issues that spring to mind that you might wish to tackle. The ability to design a good question is a skill that should be cultivated, and such questions will allow you to impress your assessor with the quality of your thinking.

> *If you construct your ideas around key questions, this will help you focus your mind and engage effectively with your subject. Your role will be like that of a detective – exploring the evidence and investigating the findings.*

Rest your case

It should be your aim to give the clear impression that your arguments are not based entirely on hunches, bias, feelings or intuition. In exams and essay questions it is usually assumed (even if not directly specified) that you will appeal to evidence to support your claims. Therefore, when you write your essay you should ensure that it is liberally sprinkled with citations and evidence. By the time the assessor reaches the end of your work, he or she should be convinced that your conclusions are evidence-based. A fatal flaw to be avoided is to make claims for which you have provided no authoritative source.

Some examples of how you might introduce your evidence and sources are provided below:

> According to Bell (1999) …
> Horwath (2003) has concluded that …
> It has been claimed by Scourfield (2002) that …
> Corby (2000) asserted that …
> A review of the evidence by Macdonald (2001) suggests that …
> Findings from a meta-analysis presented by Coren and Barlow (2002) would indicate that …

It is sensible to vary the expressions used so that you are not monotonous and repetitive, and it also aids variety to introduce researchers' names at various places in the sentence (not always at the beginning). It is advisable to choose the expression that is most appropriate – for example you can make a stronger statement about reviews that have identified recurrent and predominant trends in findings, as opposed to one study that appears to run contrary to all the rest.

Careful use of quotations

Although it is desirable to present a good range of cited sources, it is not judicious to present these as a 'patchwork quilt' – that is, you just paste together what others have said with little thought for interpretative comment or coherent structure. It is a good general point to aim to avoid very lengthy quotes – short ones can be very effective. Aim at blending the quotations as naturally as possible into the flow of your sentences. Moreover, it is good to vary your practices – sometimes use short, direct, brief quotes (cite page number as well as author and year), and at times you can summarise the gist of a quote in your own words. In this case you should cite the author's name and year of publication but leave out quotation marks and page number.

In terms of referencing, practice may vary from one discipline to the next, but some general points that will go a long way in contributing to good practice are:

- If a reference is cited in the text, it must be in the list at the end (and vice versa).
- Names and dates in the text should correspond exactly with the list in the References or Bibliography.
- List of References and Bibliography should be in alphabetical order by the surname (not the initials) of the author or first author.
- Any reference you make in the text should be traceable by the reader (they should clearly be able to identify and trace the source).
- Every institution will have guidelines on referencing which should be followed.

A clearly defined introduction

In an introduction to an essay you have the opportunity to define the problem or issue that is being addressed and to set it within context. Resist the temptation to elaborate on any issue at the introductory stage. For example, think of a music composer who throws out hints and suggestions of the motifs that the orchestra will later develop. What he or she does in the introduction is to provide little tasters of what will follow in order to whet the audience's appetite. If you go back to the analogy of the game of tennis, you can think of the introduction as marking out the boundaries of the court in which the game is to be played.

If you leave the introduction and definition of your problem until the end of your writing, you will be better placed to map out the directions that will be taken.

Conclusion – adding the finishing touches

In the conclusion you should aim to tie your essay together in a clear and coherent manner. It is your last chance to leave an overall impression in your reader's mind. Therefore, you will at this stage want to do justice to your efforts and not sell yourself short. This is your opportunity to identify where the strongest evidence points or where the balance of probability lies. The conclusion to an exam question often has to be written hurriedly under pressure of time, but with an essay (coursework) you have time to reflect on, refine and adjust the content to your satisfaction. It should be your goal to make the conclusion a smooth finish that does justice to the range of content in summary and succinct form. Do not under-estimate the value of an effective conclusion. 'Sign off' your essay in a manner that brings closure to the treatment of your subject.

The conclusion gives us the chance to demonstrate where the findings have brought us to date, to highlight the issues that remain unresolved and to point to where future research should take us.

Top-down and bottom-up clarity

An essay gives you the opportunity to refine each sentence and paragraph on your word-processor. Each sentence is like a tributary that leads into the stream of the paragraph that in turn leads into the main stream of the essay. From a 'top-down' perspective (that is, starting at the top with your major outline points), clarity can be improved by the structure you draft in your outline. You can ensure that the sub-headings are appropriately placed under the most relevant main heading, and that both sub- and main headings are arranged in logical sequence. From a 'bottom-up' perspective (that is, building up the details that 'flesh out' your main points), you should check that each sentence is a 'feeder' for the predominant concept in a given paragraph.

When all this is done you can check that the transition from one point to the next is smooth rather than abrupt.

Checklist: Summary for essay writing

✓ Before you start – have a 'warm-up' by tossing the issues around in your head.

✓ List the major concepts and link them in fluent form.

✓ Design a structure (outline) that will facilitate balance, progression, fluency and clarity.

✓ Pose questions and address these in critical fashion.

✓ Demonstrate that your arguments rest on evidence and spread cited sources across your essay.

✓ Provide an introduction that sets the scene and a conclusion that rounds off the arguments.

3.5

revision hints and tips

What this section will give you: how to –

- map out your accumulated material for revision
- choose summary tags to guide your revision
- keep well-organised folders for revision
- make use of effective memory techniques
- revise in a way that combines bullet points and in-depth reading
- profit from the benefits of revising with others
- attend to the practical exam details that will help keep panic at bay
- use strategies that keep you task-focused during the exam
- select and apply relevant points from your prepared outlines.

The return journey

Revision is a means to 'revisit' what you have encountered before. Familiarity with your material can help reduce anxiety, inspire confidence and fuel motivation for further learning and good performance.

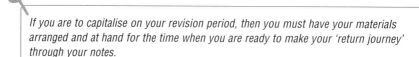

If you are to capitalise on your revision period, then you must have your materials arranged and at hand for the time when you are ready to make your 'return journey' through your notes.

Start at the beginning

Strategy for revision should be on your mind from your first lecture at the beginning of your academic term or semester. You should be like the squirrel that stores up nuts for the winter. Do not waste any lecture, tutorial, seminar, group discussion, etc., by letting the material evaporate into thin air. Get into the habit of making a few guidelines for revision after each learning activity. Keep a folder, or file, or little notebook that is reserved for revision and write out the major points that you have learned. By establishing this regular practice you will find that what you have learned becomes consolidated in your mind, and you will also be in a better position to 'import' and 'export' your material both within and across subjects.

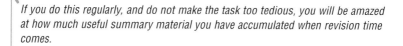

If you do this regularly, and do not make the task too tedious, you will be amazed at how much useful summary material you have accumulated when revision time comes.

Compile summary notes

It would be useful and convenient to have a little notebook or cards on which you can write outline summaries that provide you with an overview of your subject at a glance. You could also use treasury tags to hold different batches of cards together while still allowing for inserts and re-sorting. Such practical resources can easily be slipped into your pocket or bag and produced when you are on the bus or train or sitting in a traffic jam. They would also be useful if you are standing in a queue or waiting for someone who is not in a rush! A glance over your notes will consolidate your learning and will also activate your mind to think further about your subject. Therefore it would also be useful to make a note of the questions that you would like to think about in greater depth. Your primary task is to get into the habit of constructing outline notes that will be useful for revision, and a worked example is provided below.

There is a part of the mind that will continue to work on problems when you have moved on to focus on other issues. Therefore, if you feed on useful, targeted information, your mind will continue to work on 'automatic pilot' after you have 'switched off'.

Example: Part of a course on communication is the use of non-verbal communication.

Your outline revision structure for this might be as follows:

1 Aspects of non-verbal communication that run parallel with language

- pauses
- tone of voice
- inflection of voice
- speed of voice.

2 Facets of non-verbal communication related to use of body parts

- how close to stand to others
- how much to use the hands
- whether to make physical contact – e.g. touching, hugging, handshake
- extent and frequency of eye contact.

3 General features that augment communication

- use of smiles and frowns
- use of eyebrows
- expressions of boredom or interest
- dress and appearance.

Keep organised records

People who have a fulfilled career have usually developed the twin skills of time and task management. It is worth pausing to remember that you can use your academic training to prepare for your future career in this respect. Therefore, ensure that you do not fall short of your potential because these qualities have not been cultivated. One important tactic is to keep a folder for each subject and divide this topic-by-topic. You can keep your topics in the same order in which they are presented in your course lectures. Bind them together in a ring binder or folder and use subject dividers to keep them apart. Make a numbered list of the contents at the beginning of the folder, and list each topic clearly as it marks a new section in your folder. Another important practice is to place all your notes on a given topic within the appropriate section straight away, without putting it off. Notes may come from lectures, seminars, tutorials, Internet searches, personal notes, etc. It is also essential that when you remove these for consultation you return them to their 'home' immediately after use.

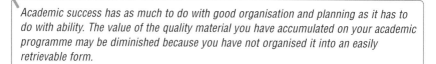

Academic success has as much to do with good organisation and planning as it has to do with ability. The value of the quality material you have accumulated on your academic programme may be diminished because you have not organised it into an easily retrievable form.

Use past papers

Revision will be very limited if it is confined to memory work. You should by all means read over your revision cards or notebook and keep the picture of the major facts in front of your mind's eye. It is also, however, essential that you become familiar with previous exam papers so that you will have some idea of how the questions are likely to be framed. Therefore, build up a good range of past exam papers (especially recent ones) and add these to your folder.

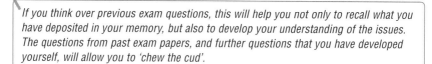

If you think over previous exam questions, this will help you not only to recall what you have deposited in your memory, but also to develop your understanding of the issues. The questions from past exam papers, and further questions that you have developed yourself, will allow you to 'chew the cud'.

Employ effective mnemonics (memory aids)

'Mnemonics' can be simply defined as aids to memory – devices that will help you recall information that might otherwise be difficult to retrieve from memory. For example, if you find an old toy in the attic of your house, it may suddenly trigger a flood of childhood memories associated with it. Mnemonics can therefore be thought of as keys that open memory's storehouse.

Visualisation is one technique that can be used to aid memory. For example, there is the *location method* by which a familiar journey is visualised and you 'place' the facts that you wish to remember at various landmarks along the journey – such as a bus stop, a car park, a shop, a store, a bend, a police station, a traffic light, etc. This has the advantage of making an association of the information you have to learn with other material that is already firmly embedded and structured in your memory. Therefore, once the relevant memory is activated, a 'domino effect' will be triggered. However, there is no reason why you cannot use a whole toolkit of mnemonics. Some examples and illustrations of these are presented below.

(i) If you can arrange your subject matter in a logical sequence this will ensure that your series of facts will also connect with each other and one will trigger the other in recall.
(ii) You can use memory devices either at the stage of initial learning or when you later return to consolidate.

Location Method – Defined above.

Visualisation – Turn information into pictures – e.g. the example given about the problems and pleasures of pets could be envisaged as two tug-of-war teams that pull against each other. You could visualise each player as an argument and have the label written on his or her t-shirt. The war could start with two players and then be joined by another two and so on. In addition you could compare each player's weight to the strength of each argument. You might also want to make use of colour – your favourite colour for the winning team and the colour you dislike most for the losers!

Alliteration's artful aid – Find a series of words that all begin with the same sounds. See the example below related to the experiments of Ebbinghaus.

Peg system – 'Hang' information onto a term so that when you hear the term you will remember the ideas connected with it (an umbrella term).

Hierarchical system – This is a development of the previous point, with higher-order, middle-order and lower-order terms. For example you could think of the continents of the world (higher order), and then group these into the countries under them (middle order). Under countries you could have cities, rivers and mountains (lower order).

Acronyms – Take the first letter of all the key words and make a word from these. An example from business is SWOT – Strengths, Weaknesses, Opportunities and Threats.

Mind-maps – These have become very popular – they allow you to draw lines that stretch out from the central idea and to develop the subsidiary ideas in the same way. It is a little like the pegging and hierarchical methods combined and turned sideways! The method has the advantage of giving you the complete picture at a glance, although they can become a complex work of art!

Rhymes and chimes – Words that rhyme and words that end with a similar sound (for example, commemoration, celebration, anticipation). These provide another dimension to memory work by including sound. Memory can be enhanced when information is processed in various modalities – such as hearing, seeing, speaking, visualising.

A confidence booster

At the end of the nineteenth century, Ebbinghaus and his assistant memorised lists of nonsense words (could not be remembered by being attached to meaning), and then endeavoured to recall these. What they discovered was:

- Some words could be recalled freely from memory, while others appeared to be forgotten.
- Words that could not be recalled were later recognised as having belonged to the lists (i.e. were not new additions).
- When the lists were jumbled into a different sequence, the experimenters were able to re-form them into the original sequence.
- When the words that were 'forgotten' were learned again, the learning process was much easier the second time (that is, there was evidence of re-learning savings).

The four points of this experiment can be remembered by alliteration: Recall, Recognition, Reconstruction and Re-learning savings. This experiment has been described as a confidence booster because it demonstrates that memory is more powerful than is often imagined, especially when we consider that Ebbinghaus and his assistant did not have the advantage of processing the meaning of the words.

Alternate between methods

It is not sufficient to present outline points in response to an exam question (although it is better to do this than nothing if you have run out of time in your exam). Your aim should be to put 'meat on the bones' by adding substance, evidence and arguments to your basic points. You should work at finding the balance between the two methods – outline revision cards might be best reserved for short bus journeys, whereas extended reading might be better employed for longer revision slots at home or in the library. Your ultimate goal should be to bring together an effective, working approach that will enable you to face your exam questions comprehensively and confidently.

In revision it is useful to alternate between scanning over your outline points, and reading through your notes, articles, chapters, etc., in an in-depth manner. Also, the use of different times, places and methods will provide you with the variety that might prevent monotony and facilitate freshness.

Revising with others

If you can find a few other students to revise with, this will provide another fresh approach to the last stages of your learning. This collective approach would allow you to assess your strengths and weaknesses (showing you where you are off-track), and to benefit from the resources and insights of others. Before you meet up you can each design some questions for the whole group to address. The group could also go through past exam papers and discuss the points that might provide an effective response to each question. It should not be the aim of the group to provide standard and identical answers for each group member to mimic. Group-work is currently deemed to be advantageous by educationalists, and team-work is held to be a desirable employability quality.

Each individual should aim to use his or her own style and content while drawing on and benefiting from the group's resources.

Checklist: Good study habits for revision time

✓ Set a date for the 'official' beginning of revision and prepare for 'revision mode'.

✓ Do not force cramming by leaving revision too late.

✓ Take breaks from revision to avoid saturation.

✓ Indulge in relaxing activities to give your mind a break from pressure.

✓ Minimise or eliminate use of alcohol during the revision season.

✓ Get into a good rhythm of sleep to allow renewal of your mind.

✓ Avoid excessive caffeine especially at night so that sleep is not disrupted.

✓ Try to adhere to regular eating patterns.

✓ Try to have a brisk walk in the fresh air each day.

✓ Avoid excessive dependence on junk food and snacks.

3.6	
exam tips	

What this section will give you: how to –

- develop strategies for controlling your nervous energy
- tackle worked examples of time and task management in exams
- attend to the practical details associated with the exam
- stay focused on the exam questions
- link revision outlines to strategy for addressing exam questions.

Handling your nerves

Exam nerves are not unusual and it has been concluded that test anxiety arises because of the perception that your performance is being evaluated, that the consequences are likely to be serious and that you are working under the pressure of a time restriction. However, it has also been asserted that the activation of the autonomic nervous system is adaptive in that it is designed to prompt us to take action in order to avoid danger. If you focus on the task in hand rather than on feeding a downward negative spiral in your thinking patterns, this will help you keep your nerves under control. In the run-up to your exams you can practise some simple relaxation techniques that will help you bring stress under control.

> *It is a very good thing if you can interpret your nervous reactions positively, but the symptoms are more likely to be problematic if you interpret them negatively, pay too much attention to them or allow them to interfere with your exam preparation or performance.*

Practices that may help reduce or buffer the effects of exam stress:

- listening to music
- going for a brisk walk
- simple breathing exercises
- some muscle relaxation
- watching a film
- enjoying some laughter
- doing some exercise
- relaxing in a bath (with music if preferred).

The best choice is going to be the one (or a combination) that works best for you – perhaps to be discovered by trial and error. Some of the above techniques can be practised on the morning of the exam, and even the memory of them can be used just before the exam. For example, you could run over a relaxing tune in your head, and have this echo inside you as you enter the exam room. The idea behind all this is, first, that stress levels must come down and, second, that relaxing thoughts will serve to displace stressful reactions. It has been said that stress is the body's call to take action, but anxiety is a maladaptive response to that call.

> *It is important you are convinced that your stress levels can come under control, and that you can have a say in this. Do not give anxiety a vacuum to work in.*

Time management with examples

The all-important matter as you approach an exam is to develop the belief that you can take control over the situation. As you work through the list of issues that you need to address, you will be able to tick them off one by one. One of the issues you will need to be clear about before the exam is the length of time you should allocate to each question. Sometimes this can be quite simple (although it is always necessary to read the rubric carefully) – for example, if two questions are to be answered in a two-hour paper, you should allow one hour for each question. If it is a two-hour paper with one essay question and five shorter answers, you could allow one hour for the essay and 12 minutes for each of the shorter questions. However, you always need to check out the weighting for the marks on each question, and you will also need to deduct whatever time it takes you to read over the paper and to choose your questions. See if you can work out a time-management strategy in each of the following scenarios. More importantly, give yourself some practice on the papers you are likely to face.

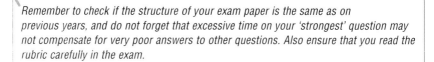

Remember to check if the structure of your exam paper is the same as on previous years, and do not forget that excessive time on your 'strongest' question may not compensate for very poor answers to other questions. Also ensure that you read the rubric carefully in the exam.

EXERCISE

Examples for working out the division of exam labour by time

1   A three-hour paper with four compulsory questions (equally weighted in marks).

2   A three-hour paper with two essays and ten short questions (each of the three sections carries one-third of the marks).

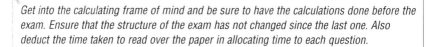

Get into the calculating frame of mind and be sure to have the calculations done before the exam. Ensure that the structure of the exam has not changed since the last one. Also deduct the time taken to read over the paper in allocating time to each question.

Suggested answers to previous exercise

1 This allows 45 minutes for each question (4 questions × 45 minutes = 3 hours). However, if you allow 40 minutes for each question this will give you 20 minutes (4 questions × 5 minutes) to read over the paper and plan your outlines.

2 *In this example you can spend 1 hour on each of the two major questions, and 1 hour on the 10 short questions. For the two major questions you could allow 10 minutes for reading and planning on each, and 50 minutes for writing. In the 10 short questions, you could allow 6 minutes in total for each (10 questions × 6 minutes = 60 minutes). However, if you allow approximately 1 minute reading and planning time, this will allow 5 minutes' writing time for each question.*

Task management with examples

After you have decided on the questions you wish to address, you then need to plan your answers. Some students prefer to plan all outlines and draft work at the beginning, while others prefer to plan and address one answer before proceeding to the next question. Decide on your strategy before you enter the exam room and stick to your plan. When you have done your draft outline as rough work, you should allocate an appropriate time for each section. This will prevent you from excessive treatment of some aspects while falling short on other parts. Such careful planning will help you achieve balance, fluency and symmetry.

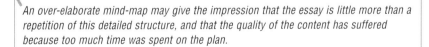

Keep awareness of time limitations and this will help you to write succinctly, keep focused on the task and prevent you dressing up your responses with unnecessary padding.

Some students put as much effort into their rough work as they do into their exam essay.

An over-elaborate mind-map may give the impression that the essay is little more than a repetition of this detailed structure, and that the quality of the content has suffered because too much time was spent on the plan.

Attend to practical details

This short section is designed to remind you of the practical details that should be attended to in preparation for an exam. There are always students who turn up late, or to the wrong venue or for the wrong exam, or do not turn up at all! Check and re-check that you have all the details of each exam correctly noted. What you don't need is to arrive late and then have to tame your panic reactions. The exam season is the time when you should aim to be at your best.

Note the following details and check that you have taken control of each one.

Checklist: practical exam details

✓   Check that you have the correct venue.

✓   Make sure you know how to locate the venue before the exam day.

✓   Ensure that the exam time you have noted is accurate.

✓   Allow sufficient time for your journey and consider the possibility of delays.

✓   Bring an adequate supply of stationery and include back-up.

✓   You may need some liquid, such as a small bottle of still water.

✓   Observe whatever exam regulations your university/college has set in place.

✓   Fill in required personal details before the exam begins.

Control wandering thoughts

In a simple study conducted in the 1960s, Ganzer (1968) found that students who frequently lifted their heads and looked away from their scripts during exams tended to perform poorly. This makes sense because it implies that the students were taking too much time out when they should have been on task. *One way to fail your exam is to get up and walk out of the test room, but another way is to 'leave' the test room mentally by being preoccupied with distracting thoughts.* The distracting thoughts may be either related to the exam itself or totally irrelevant to it. The net effect of both these forms of intrusion is to distract you from the task at hand and impair your test performance. Read over the two lists of distracting thoughts presented below.

Typical test-relevant thoughts (evaluative)

- I wish I had prepared better.
- What will the examiner think?
- Others are doing better than me.
- What I am writing is nonsense.
- Can't remember important details.

Characteristic test-irrelevant thoughts (non-evaluative)

- Looking forward to this weekend.
- Which video should I watch tonight?
- His remark really annoyed me yesterday.
- Wonder how the game will go on Saturday.
- I wonder if he/she really likes me.

Research has consistently shown that distracting, intrusive thoughts during an exam are more detrimental to performance than stressful symptoms such as sweaty palms, dry mouth, tension, trembling, etc. Moreover, it does not matter whether the distracting thoughts are negative evaluations related to the exam or are totally irrelevant to the exam. The latter may be a form of escape from the stressful situation.

Practical suggestions for controlling wandering thoughts

- Be aware that this problem is detrimental to performance.
- Do not look around to find distractions.
- If distracted, write down 'keep focused on task'.
- If distracted again, look back at above and continue to do this.
- Start to draft rough work as soon as you can.
- If you struggle with initial focus then re-read or elaborate on your rough work.
- If you have begun your essay, re-read your last paragraph (or two).
- Do not throw fuel on your distracting thoughts – starve them by re-engaging with the task at hand.

Links to revision

If you have followed the guidelines given for revision, you will be well equipped with outline plans when you enter the exam room. You may have chosen to use headings and sub-headings, mind-maps, hierarchical approaches or just a series of simple mnemonics. Whatever method you choose, you should have a series of memory triggers that will help you once you begin to write.

Although you may have clear templates with a definite structure or framework for organising your material, you will need to be flexible about how this should be applied to your exam questions.

Flight, fight or freeze

As previously noted, the autonomic nervous system (ANS) is activated when danger or apparent danger is imminent. Of course, in the case of an exam, a job interview, a driving test or a TV appearance, for example, the threat is not physical. Indeed the ANS can be activated even at the anticipation of a future threat. However, the reaction is more likely to be stronger as you enter the crucial time of testing or challenge. Symptoms may include over-breathing, trembling, headaches, nausea, tension, dry mouth and palpitations. How should we react to these once they have been triggered? A postman might decide to run away from a barking dog and run the risk of being chased and bitten. A second possible response is to freeze on the spot – this might arrest the animal in its tracks, but is no use in an exam situation. In contrast, to fight might not be the best strategy against the dog, but will be more productive in an exam. That is, you are going into the exam room to 'tackle' the questions, and not to run away from the challenge before you.

3.7

tips on interpreting essay and exam questions

What this section will give you, in addressing exam and essay questions, is how to –

- focus on the issues that are relevant and central
- read questions carefully and take account of all the words
- produce a balanced critique in your outline structures
- screen for the key words that will shape your response
- focus on different shades of meaning between 'critique', 'evaluate', 'discuss' and 'compare and contrast'.

What do you see?

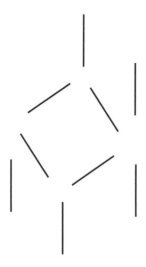

The suggested explanation for visual illusions is the inappropriate use of cues – that is, we try to interpret three-dimensional figures in the real world with the limitations of a two-dimensional screen (the retina in the eye). We use cues such as shade, texture, size, background, etc., to interpret distance, motion or shape, and we sometimes use these inappropriately. Another visual practice we engage in is to 'fill in the blanks' or join up the lines (as in the case of the nine lines above – which we might assume to be a chair). Our tendency is to impose the nearest similar and familiar template on that which we think we see. The same occurs in the social world – when we are introduced to someone of a different race we may (wrongly) assume certain things about them. The same can also apply to the way you read exam or essay questions. In these cases you are required to 'fill in the blanks', but what you fill in may be the wrong interpretation of the question. This is especially likely if you have primed yourself to expect certain questions to appear in an exam, but it can also happen in coursework essays. Although examiners do not deliberately design questions to trick you or trip you up, they cannot always ensure that you do not see things that were not designed to be there. When one student was asked what the four seasons were, the response given was, 'salt, pepper, mustard and vinegar'. This was not quite what the examiner had in mind!

A politician's answer

Politicians are renowned for refusing to answer questions directly or for evading them by raising other questions. For example, when a politician was asked, 'Is it true that you always answer questions by asking another?' the reply was, 'Who told you that?' Therefore, make sure that you answer the set question, although there may be other questions for further study that arise out of this and that you might want to highlight in your conclusion. As a first principle you must answer the set question, and not another question that you had hoped for in the exam or essay.

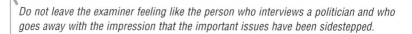

> *Do not leave the examiner feeling like the person who interviews a politician and who goes away with the impression that the important issues have been sidestepped.*

> *Be ready to resist the wealth of fascinating material at your disposal that is not directly relevant to your question.*

Missing your question

A student bitterly complained after an exam that the topic he had revised so thoroughly had not been tested in the exam. The first response to that is that students should always cover enough topics to avoid selling themselves short in the exam – the habit of 'question-spotting' is always a risky game to play. However, the reality in the anecdotal example was that the question the student was looking for was there, but he had not seen it. He had expected the question to be couched in certain words and he could not find these when he scanned over the questions in blind panic. Therefore, the simple lesson is always to read over the questions carefully, slowly and thoughtfully. This practice is time well spent.

> *You can miss the question if you restrict yourself to looking for a set form of words and if you do not read over all the words carefully.*

Write it down

If you write down the question you have chosen to address, and perhaps quietly articulate it with your lips, you are more likely to process fully its true meaning and intent. Think of how easy it is to misunderstand a question that has been put to you verbally because you have misinterpreted the tone or emphasis.

If you read over the question several times you should be aware of all the key words and will begin to sense the connections between the ideas, and will envisage the possible directions you should take in your response.

Take the following humorous example:

(a) What is that on the road ahead?
(b) What is that on the road, a head?

Question (a) calls for the identification of an object (what is that?), but question (b) has converted this into an object that suggests there has been a decapitation! Ensure, therefore, that you understand the direction the question is pointing you towards, so that you do not go off at a tangent. One word in the question that is not properly attended to can throw you completely off track – as in the following example:

(a) Discuss whether the love of money is the root of all evil.
(b) Discuss whether money is the root of all evil.

These are two completely different questions: (a) suggests that the real problem with money is inherent in faulty human use – that is, money itself may not be a bad thing if it is used as a servant and not a master; (b) on the other hand, may suggest that behind every evil act that has ever been committed money is likely to have been implicated somewhere in the motive.

Pursue a critical approach

In degree courses you are usually expected to write critically rather than merely descriptively, although it may be necessary to include some descriptive material.

Given that most questions will require some form of critical evaluation of the evidence, theory or policy, you would need to address the issues one by one from both standpoints. What you should not do is digress about irrelevant or vague information (often weak students will draw upon 'I think that … '), or common-sense arguments more suited to tabloid newspapers.

Analyse the parts

In an effective sports team the end product is always greater than the sum of the parts. Similarly, a good essay cannot be constructed without reference to the parts. Furthermore, the parts will become clear as you break down the question into the components it suggests to you. Although the breaking-down of a question into components is not sufficient for an excellent essay, it is a necessary starting point.

To achieve a good response to an exam or essay question, aim to integrate all the individual issues presented in a manner that gives shape and direction to your efforts.

❝ Trace in a critical manner western society's changing attitudes to the corporal punishment of children. ❞

In this case you might want to consider the role of governments, the Church, schools, parents and the media. However, you will need to have some reference points to the past as you are asked to address the issue of change. There would also be scope to look at where the strongest influences for change arise and where the strongest resistance comes from. You might argue that the changes have been dramatic or evolutionary.

Give yourself plenty of practice at thinking of questions in this kind of way – both with topics included or not included in your course. Topics not on your course that really interest you may be a helpful way to 'break you in' to this critical way of thinking.

Checklist: Ensure that questions are understood before being fully addressed

✓ Read over the chosen question several times.

✓ Write it down to ensure that it is clear.

✓ Check that you have not omitted any important aspect or point of emphasis.

✓ Ensure that you do not wrongly impose preconceived expectations on the question.

✓ Break the question into parts (dismantle and rebuild).

When asked to discuss

Students often ask how much of their own opinion they should include in an essay. In a discussion, when you raise one issue, another one can arise out of it. One tutor used to introduce his lectures by saying that he was going to 'unpack' the arguments. When you unpack an object (such as a new desk that has to be assembled), you first remove the overall packaging, such as a large box, and then proceed to remove the covers from all the component parts. After that you attempt to assemble all the parts, according to the given design, so that they hold together in the intended manner. In a discussion your aim should be not just to identify and define all the parts that contribute, but also to show where they fit (or don't fit) into the overall picture.

> Although the word 'discuss' implies some allowance for your opinion, remember that this should be informed opinion rather than groundless speculation. Also, there must be direction, order, structure and an end product.

Checklist: Features of a response to a 'discuss' question

✓ Contains a chain of issues that lead into each other in sequence.
✓ Clear shape and direction is unfolded in the progression of the argument.
✓ Is underpinned by reference to findings and certainties.
✓ Issues where doubt remains are identified.
✓ The tone of the argument may be tentative but should not be vague.

If a critique is requested

One example that might help clarify what is involved in a critique is the hotly debated topic of the physical punishment of children. It would be important in the interest of balance and fairness to present all sides and shades of the argument. You would then look at whether there is available evidence to support each argument, and you might introduce issues that have been coloured by prejudice, tradition, religion and legislation. It would be an aim to identify emotional arguments, arguments based on intuition, and to get down to those arguments that really have solid evidence-based support. Finally, you would want to flag up where the strongest evidence appears to lie, and you should also identify issues that appear to be inconclusive. It would be expected that you should, if possible, arrive at some certainties.

If asked to compare and contrast

When asked to compare and contrast, you should be thinking in terms of similarities and differences. You should ask what the two issues have in common, and what features of each are distinct. Your preferred strategy for tackling this might be to work first through all the similarities and then through all the contrasts (or vice versa). On the other hand, you might prefer to deal with one similarity and contrast, followed by another similarity and contrast, etc.

Example – Compare and contrast the family support and child protection policies on child abuse

Similarities

- concern for reducing abuse and neglect
- concern to help parents care for their children well
- recognition of need for state involvement in family life.

Contrasts

- degree of priority given to preserving the family v. protecting the child
- relative weight given to rights of parents and children
- boundary for state intervention – early support v. reactive to serious abuse
- views on causes of child abuse and neglect
- degree of parental responsibility for child welfare.

Whenever evaluation is requested

A worked example of evaluation – SureStart
Imagine that you have been asked to evaluate the SureStart schemes in the UK. The latest evaluative report shows some modest success but raises concerns

about whether teenage mothers are faring worse in SureStart areas. As part of your task, you might want to review past features (retrospective), such as the evidence of success in earlier schemes such as the HeadStart schemes in the USA on which SureStart is modelled. You could also look at the methods used in evaluating SureStart and consider whether they were adequate. You could consider present features – the evidence on how well the schemes are being implemented, whether they are following the basic ideas, and whether they are still at a very early stage. You might also look to the future, and envisage possible future changes, such as spreading some of the lessons from the earliest schemes to others so that they benefit from that experience.

This illustration may provoke you to think about how you might approach a question that asks you to evaluate some theory or concept in your own academic field of study. Some summary points are presented below:

- Has the theory/concept stood the test of time?
- Is there a supportive evidence base that would not easily be overturned?
- Are there questionable elements that have been or should be challenged?
- Does more recent evidence point to a need for modification?
- Is the theory/concept robust and likely to be around for the foreseeable future?
- Could it be strengthened through being merged with other theories/concepts?

EXERCISE

Write your own checklist on what you remember or understand about each of the following: 'discuss', 'compare and contrast', 'evaluate' and 'critique' (just a key word or two for each). If you find this difficult, then you should read the section again and then try the exercise.

✓ ....
✓ ....
✓ ....
✓ ....

It should be noted that the words presented in the above examples might not always be the exact words that will appear on your exam script – e.g. you might find 'analyse', or 'outline' or 'investigate', etc.

The best advice is to check over your past exam papers and familiarise yourself with the words that occur most often.

In summary, this chapter has been designed to give you reference points to measure where you are at in your studies, and to help you map out the way ahead in manageable increments. It should now be clear that learning should not merely be a mechanical exercise, such as simply memorising and reproducing study material. Quality learning also involves making connections between ideas, thinking at a deeper level by attempting to understand your material and developing a critical approach to learning. However, this cannot be achieved without the discipline of preparation for lectures, seminars and exams, or without learning to structure your material (headings and sub-headings) and to set each unit of learning within its overall context in your subject and programme. An important device in learning is to develop the ability to ask questions (whether written, spoken or silent). Another useful device in learning is to illustrate your material and use examples that will help make your study fun, memorable and vivid. It is useful to set problems for yourself that will allow you to think through solutions and therefore enhance the quality of your learning.

On the one hand there are the necessary disciplined procedures such as preparation before each learning activity and consolidation afterwards. It is also vital to keep your subject material in organised folders so that you can add/extract/replace material when you need to. On the other hand, there is the need to develop personality qualities such as feeding your confidence, fuelling your motivation and turning stress responses to your advantage. This section has presented strategies to guide you through finding the balance between these organised and dynamic aspects of academic life.

Your aim should be to become an 'all-round student' who engages in and benefits from all the learning activities available to you (lectures, seminars, tutorials, computing, labs, discussions, library work, etc.), and to develop all the academic and personal skills that will put you on the road to academic achievement. It will be motivating and confidence-building for you if you can recognise the value of these qualities, both across your academic programme and beyond graduation to the world of work. They will also serve you well in your continued commitment to life-long learning.

Further Reading

D. MCILROY (2003) *Studying at University: how to be a successful student*, London: Sage Publications.

part four

additional resources

glossary of key terms

'Achieving best evidence'   Guidance produced by the Crown Prosecution Service on how to prepare and support witnesses, including the specific concerns and provisions for children giving evidence in court.

Anti-discriminatory practice   Recognising the power imbalances in our society and working towards redressing the balance, includes identifying and challenging discriminatory prejudices.

Area Child Protection Committee   Now replaced by the Local Safeguarding Children Board, the ACPC was the inter-agency body responsible for co-ordinating child protection services in a local area and developing local inter-agency policies and procedures.

Assessment Framework   Underpinning all the assessment forms in children's services, this is an ecological framework for organising information about a child's health and development in three domains: the child's developmental needs, parenting capacity, and family and environmental factors.

'At risk'   Traditionally used to refer to a child at risk of abuse but now also used to refer to children at risk of social exclusion or at risk of failing to fulfil their potential.

Attachment theory   Based on the work of the psychoanalyst John Bowlby, this is a theory of personality development in which the nature of infants' relationships with their caregivers are considered to shape their future emotional and social competence.

Beckford, Jasmine   The 4-year-old girl whose death in 1984 led to an influential inquiry, chaired by Louis Blom-Cooper, that stressed the importance of prioritising the safety and welfare of the child over that of the parents.

CAMHS   Child and Adolescent Mental Health Services, a multi-disciplinary team that offers assessment, treatment and support for mental health problems and disorders to children and their families.

Care order   Made by a court, after assessing an application by a local authority, that authorises the removal of a child from parental care.

Child   Anyone who has not yet reached their eighteenth birthday.

'Child in need'   Defined in the Children Act 1989 as a child who is unlikely to achieve or maintain a reasonable standard of health or development without appropriate provision of services from a local authority. The category includes children who are disabled.

Child protection conference   A meeting of the relevant professionals plus family members (including the child if appropriate) where information is shared to form an assessment of whether the child is at risk of significant harm and to make plans about how to deal with any risk.

Child protection plan   If the decision is made at a child protection conference to put a child's name on the register then a child protection plan is drawn up, setting out what needs to be done and by whom to protect the child's safety and welfare.

Child protection procedures   See *Working Together to Safeguard Children.*

Child protection register   Provides a record of every child in an area for whom there are unresolved child protection concerns and who is currently the subject of an inter-agency child protection plan. The decision to place a child's name on the register is usually made at a child protection conference.

Children's Commissioner   Each country in the UK appoints a Children's Commissioner to ensure that the views and interests of children are heard and acted upon at a national level. Their legal authority varies slightly between the countries.

Children's Trust   The Children Act 2004 established Children's Trusts as the required organisational structure to bring together all services for children and young people in an area. As a key element in the drive to develop preventive services, Children's Trusts will seek to change the behaviour of those who work every day with children and families, so that those children and families experience more integrated and responsive services, where specialist support is embedded in and accessed through universal services.

Climbie, Victoria   Her death in 2000 led to the first major inquiry for some years. Chaired by Lord Laming, the findings of the inquiry on poor accountability and co-ordination of agencies fed into the government's change agenda for children's services.

Colwell, Maria   The subject of the first major child abuse inquiry in 1974. The findings of that inquiry led to the establishment of the basic framework of the child protection services that we have today.

Common Assessment Framework   A multi-agency framework for assessment, to facilitate good identification of children's needs and referral to the appropriate agencies. It should also promote the development of a common language and improve the sharing of information between agencies. It is being trialled in 12 areas during 2005/6 and should be adopted throughout England by the end of 2008.

Common Core of Skills and Knowledge

A curriculum setting out the basic skills and knowledge needed by people (including volunteers) whose work brings them into regular contact with children, young people and families. It will help multi-disciplinary teams to work together more effectively in the interests of the child.

Core assessment

In-depth assessment which addresses the central or most important aspects of the needs of a child and the capacity of his or her parents or caregivers to respond appropriately to these needs within the wider family and community context. A core assessment should be completed within 35 working days of the completion of the initial assessment, or the decision being made to initiate section 47 inquiries, or new information received on an open case indicating that a core assessment should be done. In the circumstances in which the core assessment process must address child protection issues, it must include section 47 inquiries.

Domestic violence

Violence between partners, mainly – but by no means always – male violence to women. It includes both physical and psychological abuse and can have a corrosive impact on the victim's self-esteem, making it hard for him/her to deal with it constructively.

Ecology

The study of the interrelationships between organisms and their environments. The Assessment Framework adopts an ecological approach to understanding a child's health and development.

Emergency Protection Order	Made by a court when there is a need for urgent action to protect a child.
Every Child Matters	The name of the 2003 Green Paper setting out the government's vision for children and now also commonly used to refer to the ensuing policy changes, in which the development of early recognition and response to problems is a key goal in helping all children to fulfil their potential.
Fabricated or Induced Illness	Where a parent makes up or causes symptoms in a child in order to gain medical attention.
Family Group Conference	A meeting of family members with professionals where the family is the primary planning group in deciding how to meet the child's needs.
Genogram	A diagrammatic way of describing the structure of a family, illustrating the different relationships between members.
Information Sharing Index	A database containing basic details of all children in England (e.g. name, address, age), plus the name and contact details of agencies to whom they are known. Practitioners can enter an 'indication' to show that they have information to share, have carried out an assessment, or are taking action.
Initial assessment	A brief assessment of each child referred to local authority children's social care where it is necessary to determine whether the child is in need, the nature of the services required, and whether a further, more detailed, core assessment should be done.
Integrated Children's System	An electronic case-management system for social care that is being implemented from 2006 onwards.

LAC system	Looked After Children forms to use with children who are looked after by the local authority to help assess, plan and monitor their development. They were developed in response to the recognition of the poor outcomes so many looked after children had.
Lead professional	The person who takes the lead in coordinating the contribution of various agencies to meet the needs of a child. Provides a single point of contact for the child and family.
Local Safeguarding Children Boards	Established in the Children Act 2004, they replace the Area Child Protection Committee with statutory bodies, with representatives of the key agencies in children's services, such as social care, health, education, police. The objective of LSCBs is to co-ordinate, and to ensure the effectiveness of, their member agencies in safeguarding and promoting the welfare of children.
'Looked after child'	A child in the care of the local authority.
Memorandum of Good Practice	Now replaced by the guidance 'Achieving Best Evidence' (2001), the memorandum provided guidance on conducting video interviews with children, including how to confine their answers to comply with the law of evidence.
Multi-Agency Public Protection Arrangements (MAPPA)	A national framework for the assessment and management of risk posed by serious and violent offenders.
'No order' principle	The principle in the Children Act 1989 that the court should only make an order when essential.

Parenting capacity	One of the three dimensions of a child's health and development assessed in the Assessment Framework.
Partnership with parents	The principle in the Children Act 1989 that, where possible, professionals should work in partnership with parents to help them bring up their children, using more coercive methods as little as possible.
Police protection power	Under Section 46 of the Children Act 1989, a police officer who has reasonable cause to believe that a child is at risk of significant harm can remove the child, or ensure the child cannot be removed from a safe place such as a hospital.
Rights of children	See United Nations Convention on the Rights of the Child.
Risk assessment	Estimating the likelihood of adverse outcomes for a child.
Risk management	Deciding what to do to minimise the assessed risk.
Safeguarding children	The broad aim of children's services not only to protect from harm but to promote the welfare of all children so that they are helped to fulfil their potential.
Section 17	The section of the Children Act 1989 that sets out local authorities' duty to help children in need.
Section 47	The section of the Children Act 1989 that gives local authorities the statutory duty to investigate wherever it has reasonable cause to suspect that a child who lives, or is found, in their area is suffering, or is likely to suffer, significant harm.
Serious case review	Carried out by the Local Safeguarding Children Board when a child dies, and abuse or neglect

is known or suspected to be a factor in the death. It should consider the involvement of the child and family with local agencies and conduct a review if there is cause for concern about the work done to establish whether there are lessons to be learned.

Significant harm

A key concept in the Children Act 1989 that acts as the threshold for a Section 47 inquiry and for considering the use of coercive measures if necessary.

Strategy discussion

Discussion held between relevant professionals about a referral to decide whether a Section 47 inquiry needs to be done.

Supervision order

An order made by a court with the same threshold criteria as a care order but conferring the duty on the supervisor to 'advise, assist and befriend' the supervised child.

Trafficking children

Crimes including the exploitation of children through force, coercion, threat and the use of deception. The exploitation may be sexual or involve labour exploitation.

United Nations Convention on the Rights of the Child

Built on varied legal systems and cultural traditions, the CRC is a universally agreed set of non-negotiable standards and obligations. These basic standards – also called human rights – set minimum entitlements and freedoms that should be respected by governments. See www.unicef.org/crc/for more details.

Working Together to Safeguard Children

Guidance produced by government on how agencies should work together to protect children and promote their welfare. It is the key document in child protection services and its contents should be well known by all practitioners.

scottish legal framework

Scotland has its own policy and legislation on social care and a system of Children's Hearings for making legal decisions about children. The Children (Scotland) Act 1995 is the key piece of legislation. Centred on the needs of children and their families, it defines both parental responsibilities and rights in relation to children. It sets out the duties and powers available to public authorities to support children and their families and to intervene when the child's welfare requires it. It embodies key principles which are consistent with the UN Convention on the Rights of the Child. Fundamentally, the act is founded on the principles that:

- Each child has a right to be treated as an individual.
- Each child who can form a view on matters affecting him or her has the right to express those views if he or she so wishes.
- Parents should normally be responsible for the upbringing of their children and should share that responsibility.
- Each child has the right to protection from all forms of abuse, neglect or exploitation.
- In decisions relating to protection of a child every effort should be made to keep the child in the family home.
- Any intervention by a public authority in the life of a child should be properly justified and should be supported by services from all relevant agencies working in collaboration.

The Act is divided into four main parts:

Part I deals with the responsibilities and rights of parents and guardians towards children and decisions about family matters.

Part II deals with the promotion of children's welfare by public authorities such as local authorities, and the operation of the Children's Hearings System.

Part III makes amendments to the law on adoption of children.

Part IV makes general and supplemental provision in relation to the Act.

Part I of the Children (Scotland) Act introduces a statement of parental responsibilities and rights, and outlines the court orders which may be made when parents separate and divorce.

Parental responsibilities

Section 1 of the Act provides that a child's parents have *four main responsibilities* toward the child. These are:

1 To safeguard and promote the child's health, development and welfare until the child reaches the age of 16.

2 To provide *direction* until the child reaches 16 and to provide *guidance* until the child reaches 18.

3 To maintain regular contact with the child until he or she is 16.

4 To act as legal representative until the child is 16.

Where there is a breach of these responsibilities a child, or their representative, will be entitled to sue. Parents, however, must comply with these responsibilities only in so far as it is 'practicable' to do so and in the 'interests of the child'.

Parental rights

Section 2 of the Act provides parents *four main rights* in order to allow them to fulfil these responsibilities. These are as follows:

1 To regulate the under-16 child's residence.

2 To *direct* and *guide* the child's upbringing.

3 To maintain contact.

4 To act as legal representative.

Part II of the Act introduces significant changes in provisions for the protection of children at risk. The Act introduces three new court orders designed to protect children from harm or the risk of harm.

Child Protection Order

The *Child Protection Order* replaces the existing provisions governing the removal of children from home where they are in danger. The Act allows anyone to apply to a sheriff for a Child Protection Order, and the sheriff may make such an order if he is satisfied that there are reasonable grounds to believe that the child

- is suffering significant harm because of ill-treatment or neglect;
- will suffer such harm if he or she is not removed to, or allowed to remain in, a place of safety.

The Child Protection Order is focused firmly on the individual needs of the child. Subject to any conditions imposed by the sheriff, it may

- require any person in a position to do so to produce the child;
- authorise the child's removal to a place of safety; or
- authorise the prevention of the child's removal where he is already in a place of safety.

Parents and the child will have an early opportunity to have the order set aside or varied by the *Exclusion Order*.

The *Exclusion Order* is an innovative measure, designed to reduce disruption and distress to children who may already have suffered physical or mental abuse. It can be obtained from the sheriff on broadly the same criteria as for a Child Protection Order. If granted, the order would require the person to whom the harm (or potential harm) is attributed to leave the family home or not to visit it, if he lives elsewhere. This is an alternative to removing the child from the security of his or her home under a Child Protection Order. Exclusion may take place at once but, as in the case of a Child Protection Order, provision is made for early review of the order by a sheriff.

Child Assessment Order

If there is good reason to suspect that a child may be suffering harm and parents refuse to allow the child to be seen in order to resolve those suspicions, a sheriff can make a *Child Assessment Order*, which gives the local authority a legal right to see and assess the child, or arrange for the child to be assessed by other professionals, such as a doctor or psychiatrist. The order may last for up to seven days and will not normally require the child's removal from his or her family home unless there is clear evidence that this is necessary. Such an application has to be determined within three working days.

references

Abel, G. and Rouleau, J. (1990) 'The nature and extent of sexual assault', in W. Marchall, D. Laws and H. Barbaree (eds), *Handbook of Sexual Assault: issues, theories and treatment of the offender*, New York: Plenum.

Aldridge, M. and Wood, J. (1998) *Interviewing Children: a guide for child care and forensic practitioners,* Chichester: Wiley.

Allsop, M. and Stevenson, O. (1995) 'Social workers' perceptions of risk in child protection, ESRC project' (a discussion paper), Nottingham: Nottingham University.

Bandura, A. (1971) *Social Learning Theory,* Morristown, NJ: General Learning.

Barbaree, H., Marshall, W. and Hudson, S. (eds) (1993) *The Juvenile Sex Offender*, New York: Guilford Press.

Barlow, J. (1997) 'Systematic review of the effectiveness of parent-training programmes in improving behaviour problems in children aged 3–10 years'. Available from www.campbellcollaboration.org.

Barn, R. (1990) 'Black children in local authority care: admission patterns', *New Community*, 16: 229–46.

Bell, M. (1999) *Child Protection: families and the conference process*, Andover: Ashgate.

Bell, M. (2002) 'Promoting children's rights through the use of relationship', *Child and Family Social Work*, 7: 1–11.

Berliner, L. and Conte, J. (1990) 'The process of victimization: the victim's perspective', *Child Abuse and Neglect*, 14: 29–40.

Biehal, N. (2006) *Reuniting Looked-after Children with their Families*, York: Joseph Rowntree Foundation, Available from www.jrf.org.uk/knowledge/findings/socialpolicy/0056.asp.

Birchall, E. and Hallett, C. (1995) *Working Together in Child Protection,* London: HMSO.

Birmingham City Council (1980) *Report of the Director of Social Services to the Social Services Committee,* Birmingham: Birmingham City Council.

Bowlby, J. (1979) *The Making and Breaking of Affectional Bonds*, London: Tavistock.

Briere, J. and Runtz, M. (1989) 'The Trauma Symptoms Checklist: early data on a new scale', *Journal of Interpersonal Violence*, 4: 151–63.

Briggs, F. and Hawkins, R. (1996) *Child Protection: a guide for teachers and child care professionals,* St Leonards: Allen & Unwin.

Brown, J., Cohen, P., Johnson, J. and Salzinger, S. (1998) 'A longitudinal analysis of risk factors for child maltreatment: findings of a 17-year prospective study of officially recorded and self-reported child abuse and neglect', *Child Abuse and Neglect*, 14: 357–64.

Browne, A. and Finkelhor, D. (1986) 'Impact of child sexual abuse: a review of the research', *Psychological Bulletin*, 99: 66–77.

Browne, K. and Lynch, M. (1998) 'The challenge of child neglect', *Child Abuse Review*, 7 (2): 73–6.

Buchanan, A. (1996) *Cycles of Child Maltreatment: facts, fallacies and interventions*, Chichester: Wiley.

Buckley, H. (2003) *Child Protection Work: beyond the rhetoric*, London: Jessica Kingsley.

Burnett, B. (1993) 'The psychological abuse of latency age children: a survey', *Child Abuse and Neglect*, 17: 441–54.

Cawson, P., Wattam, C., Brooker, S. and Kelly, G. (2000) *Child Maltreatment in the United Kingdom: a study of the prevalence of child abuse and neglect*, London: NSPCC.

Chaffin, M. and Friedrich, B. (2004) 'Evidence-based treatments in child abuse and neglect', *Children and Youth Services Review*, 26: 1097–1113.

Chaffin, M., Silovsky, J., Funderburk, B., Valle, L., Brestan, E., Balachova, T. et al. (2004) 'Parent–child interaction therapy with physically abusive parents: efficacy for reducing future abuse reports', *Journal of Consulting and Clinical Psychology*, 72: 491–9.

Chambless, D. and Ollendick, T. (2001) 'Empirically supported psychological interventions: controversies and practices', *Annual Review of Psychology*, 52: 685–716.

Chand, A. (2000) 'The over-representation of Black children in the child protection system: possible causes, consequences and solutions', *Child and Family Social Work*, 5: 67–78.

Cleaver, H., Unell, I. and Aldgate, J. (1999) *Children's Needs – Parenting Capacity: the impact of parental mental illness, problem alcohol and drug use, and domestic violence on children's development*, London: HMSO.

Cleaver, H., Walker, S. with Meadows, P. (2004) *Assessing Children's Needs and Circumstances: the impact of the assessment framework,* London: Jessica Kingsley.

Cohen, J. and Mannarino, A. (1997) 'A treatment study of sexually abused preschool children: outcome during a one year follow-up', *Journal of the Academy of Child and Adolescent Psychiatry*, 36: 1228–35.

Coohey, C. (1995) 'Neglectful mothers, their mothers and partners: the significance of mutual aid', *Child Abuse and Neglect*, 19 (8): 885–95.

Cooper, A., Hetherington, R. and Katz, I. (2003) *The Risk Factor: making the child protection system work for children,* London: Demos. Available to download from www.demos.co.uk.

Corby, B. (1987) *Working with Child Abuse*. Milton Keynes: Open University Press.

Corby, B. (2000) *Child Abuse: towards a knowledge base*, 2nd edn, Buckingham: Open University Press.

Coren, E. and Barlow, J. (2002) 'Systematic review of individual and group-based parenting programmes for improving psychosocial outcomes for teenage parents and their children'. Available from www.campbellcollaboration.org.

Creighton, S. (2004) *Prevalence and Incidence of Child Abuse: international comparisons*, London: NSPCC Research Department.

Crittenden, P. (1988) 'Distorted patterns of relationship in maltreating families: the role of internal representation models,' *Journal of Reproductive and Infant Psychology*, 6: 183–99.

Dale, P. (2004) '"Like a fish in a bowl": parents' perceptions of child protection services', *Child Abuse Review*, 13: 137–57.

Dale, P., Green, R. and Fellows, R. (2006) *Child Protection Assessment Following Serious Injuries to Infants*, Chichester: Wiley.

Department for Education and Skills (DfES) (2005) *Common Core of Skills and Knowledge for the Children's Workforce*, London: DfES.

Department for Education and Skills (DfES) (2006a) *Common Assessment Framework*. London: DfES.

Department for Education and Skills (DfES) (2006b) *Working Together to Safeguard Children*, London: DfES.

Department of Health (1988) *Report of the Inquiry into Child Abuse in Cleveland, 1987*, London: HMSO.

Department of Health (1995) *Child Protection: messages from research*, London: HMSO.

Department of Health (2000) *Framework for the Assessment of Children in Need and Their Families*, London: HMSO.

Department of Health (2003) *What to Do if You're Worried a Child is Being Abused*, London: Department of Health.

Department of Health and Human Services (DHHS) (1993) *A Report on the Maltreatment of Children with Disabilities*, Washington, DC: Government Printing Office.

Department of Health and Human Services (DHHS) (1998) *Child Maltreatment 1996: reports from the states to the National Child Abuse and Neglect Data System*, Washington, DC: Government Printing Office.

Department of Health and Social Security (DHSS) (1974) *Report of the Committee of Inquiry into the Care and Supervision Provided in Relation to Maria Colwell*, London: HMSO.

Dingwall, R. (1989) 'Some problems about predicting child abuse and neglect', in O. Stevenson (ed.), *Child Abuse: professional practice and public policy*, London: Harvester Wheatsheaf.

Dobash, R. and Dobash, R. (1979) *Violence against Wives: a case against patriarchy*, London: Open Books.

Dobash, R. and Dobash, R. (1987) 'Violence towards wives', In J. Orford (ed.), *Coping with Disorders in the Family*, Surrey: Guildford Press.

Dodge, K., Bates, J. and Petit, G. (1990) 'Mechanisms in the cycle of violence', *Science*, 250: 1678–83.

Drake, B. and Pandey, S. (1996) 'Understanding the relationship between neighbourhood poverty and specific types of child maltreatment', *Child Abuse and Neglect,* 20: 1003–1018.

Driver, E. and Droisen, A. (1989) *Child Sexual Abuse: feminist perspectives,* London: Macmillan.

ECPAT International (2005) *Violence against Children in Cyberspace,* Bangkok: End Child Prostitution And Trafficking (ECPAT) International.

Egeland, B. (1993) 'A history of abuse is a major risk factor for abusing the next generation', in R. Gelles and D. Loseke (eds), *Current Controversies on Family Violence*, Newbury Park, CA: Sage Publications.

Ellaway, B., Payne, E., Rolfe, K., Dunstan, F., Kemp, A., Butler I. and Sibert, J. (2004) 'Are abused babies protected from further abuse?' *Archives of Diseases of Childhood*, 89: 845–6.

Elliott, F. (1988) 'Neurological factors', In V. Van Hasselt, R. Morison, S. Bellack and M. Heresen (eds), *Handbook of Family Violence*, New York: Plenum.

English, D., Graham, J., Litrownik, A., Everson, M. and Bangdiwala, S. (in press) 'Defining maltreatment chronicity: are there differences in child outcomes?' *Children and Youth Services Review*.

Erickson M. and Egeland B. (1996) 'Child neglect', in J. Briere, L. Berliner, J. Bulkley, C. Jenny and T. Reid (eds), *The APSAC Handbook of Child Maltreatment*, Thousand Oaks, CA: Sage Publications.

Esping-Anderson, G. (1990) *Three Worlds of Welfare Capitalism*, Princeton: Princeton University Press.

Family Rights Group (2002) *Family Group Conferences: principles and practice guidance*, Barkingside, Essex: Barnardo's. Available from www.barnardos. org.uk.

Farmer, E. and Owen, M. (1995) *Child Protection Practice: private risks and public remedies*, London: HMSO.

Fergusson, D. and Mullen, P. (1999) *Childhood Sexual Abuse: an evidence based perspective*, Thousand Oaks, CA: Sage Publications.

Ferguson, H. (2005) 'Working with violence, the emotions and the psycho-social dimensions of child protection: reflections on the Victoria Climbie case', *Social Work Education*, 24 (7): 781–95.

Ferri, E., Bynner, J. and Wadsworth, M. (eds) (2003) *Changing Britain, Changing Lives: three generations at the turn of the century*, London: Institute of Education.

Finkelhor, D. (1981) 'The sexual abuse of boys', *Victimology: An International Journal*, 6: 76–84.

Finkelhor, D. (1993) 'Epidemiological factors in the clinical identification of child sexual abuse', *Child Abuse and Neglect*, 17: 67–70.

Finkelhor, D. (1994) 'The international epidemiology of child sexual abuse', *Child Abuse and Neglect*, 18: 409–17.

Finkelhor, D. and Lewis, I. (1988) 'An epidemiological approach to the study of child molestation', *Annals of the New York Academy of Sciences*, 528: 64–78.

Finkelhor, D., Hotaling, G., Lewis, I. and Smith, C. (1990) 'Sexual abuse in a national survey of adult men and women: prevalence, characteristics and risk factors', *Child Abuse and Neglect*, 14: 19–28.

Fook, J. (2002) *Social Work: critical theory and practice*, London: Sage Publications.

Gambrill, E. (2003) 'Evidence based practice: sea change or the emperor's new clothes?' *Journal of Social Work Education*, 39: 3–23.

Gambrill, E. (2006) *Social Work Practice: a critical thinker's guide*, 2nd edn, Oxford: Oxford University Press.

Ganzer, V. J. (1968) 'Effects of audience presence and test anxiety on learning and retention in a serial learning situation', *Journal of Personality and Social Psychology*, 8: 194–9.

Garbarino, J., Gutterman, E. and Seeley, J. (1986) *The Psychologically Battered Child*, San Francisco, CA: Jossey-Bass.

Geddes, J. and Plunkett, J. (2004) 'The evidence base for shaken baby syndrome', *British Medical Journal*, 328: 719–20.

Gelles, R. (1973) 'Child abuse as psychopathology: a sociological critique and reformulation', *American Journal of Orthopsychiatry*, 43: 611–21.

Gelles, R. and Cornell, C. (1990) *Intimate Violence in Families*, Beverly Hills, CA, Sage Publications.

Gelles R. and Strauss, M. (1988) *Intimate Violence,* New York: Simon & Schuster.

Giardino, A. and Giardino, E. (2002) *Recognition of Child Abuse for the Mandated Reporter*, St Louis, MI: G.W. Medical Publishing, Inc.

Gibbs, L. and Gambrill, E. (1999) *Critical Thinking for Social Workers: exercises for the helping professions,* Thousand Oaks, CA: Pine Forge Press.

Goodman, R. (1997) 'The Strengths and Difficulties Questionnaire: a research note', *Journal of Child Psychology and Psychiatry*, 38: 581–6.

Goodman, R., Meltzer, H. and Bailey, V. (1998) 'The Strengths and Difficulties Questionnaire: a pilot study on the validity of the self-report version', *European Child and Adolescent Psychiatry*, 7: 125–30.

Gorey, K. and Leslie, D. (1997) 'The prevalence of child sexual abuse: integrative review and adjustment for potential response and measurement biases', *Child Abuse and Neglect*, 21: 391–8.

Gough, D. (1997) *Child Abuse Interventions: a review of the research literature*, London: HMSO.

Gough, D. (2003) 'Research for practice in child neglect', in J. Taylor and B. Daniel (eds), *Child Neglect: practice issues for health and social care,* London: Jessica Kingsley.

Hagall, A. (1998) *Dangerous Care: reviewing the risks to children from their carers,* London: Bridge Child Care Development Service.

Hammond, K. (1996) *Human Judgement and Social Policy: irreducible uncertainty, inevitable error, unavoidable injustice*, Oxford: Oxford University Press.

Hardiker, P., Exton, K. and Barker, M. (1991) *Policies and Practices in Preventive Child Care*, London: Avebury/Gower.

Hart, S., Brassard, M., Binggeli, N. and Davidson, H. (2002) 'Psychological maltreatment', in *The APSAC Handbook on Child Maltreatment*, J. Myers, L. Berliner, J. Briere, C. Hendrix, C. Jenny and T. Reid (eds), New York: Sage Publications.

Hazelrigg, M., Cooper, H. and Bourduin, C. (1987) 'Evaluating the effectiveness of family therapies: an integrative review and analysis', *Psychological Bulletin*, 101 (3): 428–42.

Herrenkohl, R. (2005) 'The definition of child maltreatment: from case study to construct', *Child Abuse and Neglect*, 29: 413–24.

Hetherington, R. (2002) 'Learning from difference: comparing child welfare systems'. Available from www.wlu.ca/documents/7203/Hetherington_ Keynote_ Address.pdf.

Hewitt, S. (1998) *Small Voices: assessing allegations of sexual abuse in preschool children,* Thousand Oaks, CA: Sage Publications.

High Court of Justice Family Division (2006) *Approved Judgment*, Neutral Citation Number [2005] EWHC 31 (Fam).

HM Government (2006) *Information Sharing: Practitioners' Guidance*, London: DfES.

Home Office (2001) *Achieving Best Evidence in Criminal Proceedings*, London: Home Office.

Home Office (2005) *Good Practice Guidance for Search Service Providers and Advice to the Public on How to Search Safely,* London: Home Office.

Home Office & Department of Health (2002) *Complex Child Abuse Investigations: inter-agency issues,* London: Home Office.

Horwath, J. (2003) 'Is this child neglect?' in J. Taylor and B. Daniel (eds), *Child Neglect: practice issues for health and social care,* London: Jessica Kingsley.

Howe, D. (2005) *Child Abuse and Neglect: attachment, development and intervention*, Basingstoke: Palgrave Macmillan.

Humphreys, C. and Mullender, A. (2005) *'Children and domestic violence: a research overview of the impact on children'*, Dartington: Research in Practice. Available from www.rip.org.uk.

Iwaniec, D. (2004) *Children Who Fail to Thrive: a practice guide*, Chichester: Wiley.

Iwaniec, D., Larkin, E. and Higgins, S. (2006) 'Research review: risk and resilience in cases of emotional abuse', *Child and Family Social Work*, 11: 73–82.

Johnson, W. (1996) 'Risk assessment research: progress and future directions', *Protecting Children*, 12: 14–19.

Kaufman, J. and Zigler, E. (1987) 'Do abused children become abusive parents?' *American Journal of Orthopsychiatry*, 57: 186–92.

Kempe, H. (1962) 'The battered child syndrome', *Journal of the American Medical Association*, 181: 17–24.

King, M. and Piper, C. (1995) *How the Law Thinks about Children*, Aldershot: Ashgate.

Kolb, D. (1984) *Experiential Learning*, Englewood Cliffs, NJ: Prentice-Hall.

La Fontaine, J. (1998) *Speak of the Devil: tales of satanic abuse in contemporary England*, Cambridge: Cambridge University Press.

Laming, Lord (2003) *The Victoria Climbie Inquiry*, London: HMSO.

Langevin, R. (1993) 'A comparison of neuroendocrine and genetic factors in homosexuality and in pedophilia', *Annals of Sex Research*, 6: 67–76.

Littell, J., Popa, M. and Forsythe, B. (2005) 'Multisystemic therapy for social, emotional and behavioural problems in youth aged 10–17', Campbell Collaboration Systematic Review, available from www.campbellcollaboration.org.

London Borough of Brent (1985*) A Child in Trust: the report of the panel of inquiry into the circumstances surrounding the death of Jasmine Beckford*, London: London Borough of Brent.

London Child Protection Committee (CPC) (2002) *London Child Protection Procedures*, London: London CPC.

Lyons, P., Doueck, H. and Wodarski, J. (1996) 'Risk assessment for child protective services: a review of the empirical literature on instrument performance', *Social Work Research*, 20: 143–55.

Macdonald, G. (2001) *Effective Interventions for Child Abuse and Neglect: an evidence-based approach to planning and evaluating interventions*, Chichester: Wiley.

MacMillan, H., MacMillan, J., Offord, D., Griffith, L. and MacMillan, A. (1994) 'Primary prevention of child physical abuse and neglect: a critical review – Part 1', *Journal of Child Psychological Psychiatry*, 35: 835–56.

MacMillan, H., Thomas, B., Jamieson, E., Walsh, C., Boyle, M., Shannon, H. and Gafni, A. (2005) 'Effectiveness of home visitation by public-health nurses in prevention of the recurrence of child physical abuse and neglect: a randomised controlled trial, *Lancet*, published online 5 May 2005.

Maguire, S., Mann, M., Sibert, J. and Kemp, A. (2005) 'Are there patterns of bruising in childhood which are diagnostic or suggestive of abuse? A systematic review', *Archives of Diseases in Childhood*, 90: 182–6.

Malinosky-Rummell, R. and Hansen, D. (1993) 'Long-term consequences of childhood physical abuse', *Psychological Bulletin*, 114: 68–79.

McCord, J. (1992) 'The Cambridge-Somerville study: a pioneering longitudinal-experimental study of delinquency prevention', in J. McCord and R. Tremblay (eds), *Preventing Antisocial Behaviour: interventions from birth, through adolescence,* New York: Guilford Press.

McGee, R. and Wolfe, D. (1991) 'Psychological maltreatment: toward an operational definition', *Development and Psychopathology*, 3: 3–18.

MAMA (Mothers against Munchausen Syndrome by Proxy Allegations) www.msbp.com. Accessed 31 March 2006.

Marziali, E., Damianakis, T. and Trocme, N. (2003) 'Nature and consequences of personality problems in maltreating caregivers', *Families in Society*, 530–8. Obtainable from www.familiesinsociety.org.

Maslach, C., Schaufeli, W. and Leiter, M. (2001) 'Job burnout', *Annual Review of Psychology*, 52: 397–422.

Mattinson, J. and Sinclair, I. (1987) *Mate and Stalemate*, Blackwell: Oxford.

Meadows, R. (ed.) (1997) *ABC of Child Abuse*, London: BMJ Publishing.

Merton, R. (1938) 'Social structure and anomie', *American Sociological Review*, 3: 672–82.

Metropolitan Police (2001) *Enough is Enough: domestic violence strategy*, London: Metropolitan Police.

Mian, M., Marton, P. and LeBaron, D. (1996) 'The effects of sexual abuse on 3- to 5-year-old girls', *Child Abuse and Neglect*, 20: 731–45.

Milne, R. and Bull, R. (1999) *Investigative Interviewing: psychology and practice*, Chichester: Wiley.

Milner, J. (1998) 'Individual and family characteristics associated with intrafamilial child physical and sexual abuse', in P. Trickett and C. Schellenbach (eds), *Violence against Children in the Family and the Community*, Washington, DC: American Psychological Association.

Milner, J. and Chilamkurti, C. (1991) 'Physical child abuse perpetrator characteristics': a review of the literature', *Journal of Interpersonal Violence*, 6: 336–44.

Monteleone, J. and Brodeur, A. (1998) *Child Maltreatment*, London: Harcourt Brace.

Mullen, P. and Fleming, J. (1998) 'Long-term effects of child sexual abuse', *Issues in Child Abuse Prevention*, 9, Melbourne: Australian Institute of Family Studies.

Mullender, A. (1996) *Rethinking Domestic Violence: the social work and probation response,* London: Routledge.

Munro, E. (1998) *Understanding Social Work: an empirical approach*, London: Continuum.

Munro, E. (1999) 'Common errors of reasoning in child protection work', *Child Abuse and Neglect*, 23 (8): 745–58.

Munro, E. (2002) *Effective Child Protection*, London: Sage Publications.

Munro, E. (2004) 'A simpler way to understand the results of risk assessment instruments', *Children and Youth Services Review*, 26 (9): 877–83.

National Commission of Inquiry into the Prevention of Child Abuse (1996) *Childhood Matters*, Vol. 1, London: HMSO.

National Institute of Neurological Disorders and Stroke (2001) 'NINDS Shaken Baby Syndrome Information Page'. Available at www.ninds.nih.gov.

Newman, T., Moseley, A., Tierney, S. and Ellis, A. (2005) *Evidence-based Social Work: a guide for the perplexed,* Lyme Regis: Russell House Publishing.

Oates, R. (1996) *The Spectrum of Child Abuse: asssessment, treatment and prevention*, New York: Brunner/Mazel.

Office for Victims of Crime (OVC) (2004) 'Child physical and sexual abuse: guidelines for treatment'. Available from www.musc.edu/cvc/.

Parkinson, P. and Humphries, C. (1998) 'Children who witness domestic violence – the implications for child protection', *Child and Family Law Quarterly*, 10: 147–59.

Parton, N. (1991) *Governing the Family: child care, child protection and the state*, London: Palgrave Macmillan.

Parton, N. (2005) *Safeguarding Childhood: early intervention and surveillance in a late modern society*, Basingstoke: Palgrave Macmillan.

Parton, N. and Wattam, C. (eds) (1999) *Child Sexual Abuse: responding to the experiences of children*, Chichester: Wiley.

Patterson, G. and Forgatch, M. (1985) 'Initiation and maintenance of process disrupting single-mother families', In G. Patterson (ed.), *Depression and Aggression in Family Interaction*, Hillsdale, NJ: Lawrence Erlbaum.

Peters, R. and Barlow, J. (2003) 'Systematic review of instruments designed to predict child maltreatment during the antenatal and postnatal periods', *Child Abuse Review*, 12: 416–39.

Polansky, N., Gaudin, J., Ammons, P. and Davis, K. (1985) 'Assessing adequacy of rearing: an urban scale', *Child Welfare*, 57: 439–48.

Ramsey, J., Rivas, C. and Feder, G. (2005) *Interventions to Reduce Violence and Promote the Physical and Psychosocial Well-being of Women who Experience Partner Violence: a systematic review of controlled evaluations,* London: Queen Mary's School of Medicine and Dentistry.

Reder, P. and Duncan, S. (1999) *Lost Innocents: a follow-up study of fatal child abuse*, London: Routledge.

Reder, P., Duncan, S. and Gray, M. (1993) *Beyond Blame: child abuse tragedies revisited,* London: Routledge.

Research in Practice (2006) *Firm Foundations. A practical guide to organisational support for the use of research evidence,* Dartington: Research in Practice.

Richardson, M. (2003) 'A personal reflective account: the impact of the collation and sharing of information during the course of a child protection investigation', *Child and Family Social Work*, 8: 123–32.

Rose, S. and Meezan, W. (1996) 'Variations in Perceptions of Child Neglect', *Child Welfare*, LXXV (2): 139–60.

Scourfield, J. (2001) 'Constructing women in child protection work', *Child and Family Social Work*, 6: 77–88.

Scourfield, J. (2002) *Gender and Child Protection*, Basingstoke: Palgrave/Macmillan.

Seebohm Committee (1968) *Report of the Committee on Local Authority and Allied Personal Social Services*, Cmnd. 412, London: HMSO.

Shemmings, D. (2000) 'Professionals' attitudes to children's participation in decision-making: dichotomous accounts and doctrinal contents', *Child and Family Social Work*, 5: 235–44.

Sidebotham, P. (2003) 'Red skies, risk factors, and early indicators', *Child Abuse Review*, 12 (1): 41–5.

Smith, M. and Fong, R. (2004) *The Children of Neglect: when no one cares*, New York: Brunner-Routledge.

Smith, J. and Rachman, S. (1984) 'Non-accidental injury to children. II – A controlled evaluation of a behaviour management programme', *Behaviour Research and Therapy*, 22 (4): 349–66.

Social Care Institute for Excellence (SCIE) (2006) *Research Briefing 6: Parenting capacity and substance misuse,* London: SCIE. Available from www.scie.org.uk.

Southall, D., Banks, M., Falkov, A. and Samuels, M. (1997) 'Covert video recordings of life-threatening child abuse: lessons for child protection', *Pediatrics*, 100: 735–60.

Spencer, N. and Baldwin, N. (2003) 'Economic, cultural and social contexts of neglect', in J. Taylor and B. Daniel (eds), *Child Neglect: practice issues for health and social care.* London: Jessica Kingsley.

Stevenson, O. (1998) *Neglected Children: issues and dilemmas,* Oxford: Blackwell Science.

Strauss, M. and Gelles, R. (eds) (1990) *Physical Violence in American Families,* New Brunswick, NJ: Transaction Books.

Strauss, M., Gelles, R. and Steinmetz, S. (1980) *Behind Closed Doors Violence in the American Family.* New York: Ancho.

Strauss, M., Hamby, S., Finkelhor, D., Moore, D. and Runyan, D. (1998) 'Identification of child maltreatment with the parent–child conflict tactic scales: development and psychometric data for a national sample of American parents', *Child Abuse and Neglect*, 22: 249–70.

Sullivan, P. and Knutson, J. (2000) 'Maltreatment and disabilities: a population-based epidemiological study', *Child Abuse and Neglect*, 24: 1257–74.

Sundell, K. and Vinnerljung, B. (2004) 'Outcomes of family group conferencing in Sweden: a 3-year follow-up', *Child Abuse and Neglect*, 28: 267–87.

SureStart (2005) *National Evaluation Report 13*, London: Institute for the Study of Children.

Taylor, J. and Daniel, B. (eds) (2003) *Child Neglect: practice issues for health and social care*, London: Jessica Kingsley.

Thoburn, J., Lewis, A. and Shemmings, D. (1995) *Paternalism or Partnership? Family involvement in child protection*, London: HMSO.

Thorpe, D. and Bilson, A. (1998) 'From protection to concern: child protection careers without apologies', *Children and Society*, 12: 373–86.

Treasury, The (2003) *Every Child Matters: change for children,* London: HMSO.

Tripodi, T. (1974) *Uses and Abuses of Social Research in Social Work*, New York: Columbia University Press.

Tunnard, J. (2002) *'Parental drug misuse – a review of impact and intervention studies'*. Available from Research in Practice: www.rip.org.uk.

Tunnard, J. (2003) *'Parental mental health problems: messages from research, policy and practice'*. Available from Research in Practice: www.rip.org.uk.

Twentyman, C. and Plotkin, R. (1982) 'Unrealistic expectations of parents who maltreat their children: an educational deficit that pertains to child development', *Journal of Clinical Psychology*, 38: 497–503.

Wall, N. (2000) *A Handbook for Expert Witnesses in Children Act Cases*, Bristol: Jordan.

Wandsworth Area Child Protection Committee (1989) *The Report of the Stephanie Fox Practice Review,* London: London Borough of Wandsworth.

Widom, K. (1989) 'Does violence beget violence? A critical examination of the literature', *Psychological Bulletin*, 106: 3–28.

Williams, L. and Finkelhor D. (1990) 'The characteristics of incestuous fathers: a review of recent studies', In W. Marshall, D. Laws and H. Barbaree (eds), *Handbook of Sexual Assault: issues, theories and treatment of the offender*, New York: Plenum.

Wilson, S., Kuebli, J. and Hughes, H. (2005) 'Patterns of maternal behaviour among neglectful families: implications for research and intervention', *Child Abuse and Neglect*, 29: 985–1001.

Winnicot, D. (1953*) 'Transitional objects and transitional phenomena' International Journal of Psychoanalysis* 34: 89–97.

Wolfe, D. (1985) 'Child abusive parents: an empirical review and analysis', *Psychological Bulletin*, 97: 462–82.

Wolfe, D. (1999) *Child Abuse: implications for child development and psychopathology,* London: Sage Publications.

Wolfner, G. and Gelles, R. (1993) 'A profile of violence towards children: a national study', *Child Abuse and Neglect*, 17: 197–212.

Yllo, K. (1993) 'Through a feminist lens: gender, power and violence', in R. Gelles and D. Loseke (eds), *Current Controversies on Family Violence*, Newbury Park, CA: Sage Publications.

Zuravin, S. and DiBlasio, F. (1992) 'Child-neglecting adolescent mothers: how do they differ from their nonmaltreating counterparts?' *Journal of Interpersonal Violence*, 7: 471–87.

index